Oxford University Press, Ely House, London W. 1

GLASGOW NEW YORK TORONTO MELBOURNE WELLINGTON
CAPE TOWN SALISBURY IBADAN NAIROBI DAR ES SALAAM LUSAKA ADDIS ABABA
BOMBAY CALCUTTA MADRAS KARACHI LAHORE DACCA
KUALA LUMPUR SINGAPORE HONG KONG TOKYO

PRINTED IN GREAT BRITAIN
AT THE UNIVERSITY PRESS, OXFORD
BY VIVIAN RIDLER
PRINTER TO THE UNIVERSITY

OXFORD THEOLOGICAL MONOGRAPHS

Oxford Theological Monographs

——

CANONS OF THE COUNCIL OF SARDICA
A.D. 343
A Landmark in the Early Development of Canon Law
By HAMILTON HESS. 1958

THE NEW TEMPLE
The Church in the New Testament
By R. J. MCKELVEY. 1968

NEW LITURGICAL FEASTS
IN LATER MEDIEVAL ENGLAND
By R. W. PFAFF. 1970

THE LEONINE
SACRAMENTARY

*A Reassessment of
its Nature and Purpose*

BY

D. M. HOPE

OXFORD UNIVERSITY PRESS

1971

PREFACE

IN spite of the complexity of the subject, it is imperative in these
days that, so far as is possible, the evolution and development
of the Christian liturgy be appreciated and understood by the
individual believer; for ultimately the liturgy is the means by
which, and the framework within which, the Christian lives out
his day-to-day existence. On the part of every Christian, therefore, one would expect some acquaintance with the historical
and social aspects of liturgical change and development, and
a rudimentary understanding of the principles of liturgical
worship, against which contemporary movements might be
informatively viewed. It has long been acknowledged that much
of the early history and development of the Western liturgy
is tenuous and obscure. It is perhaps surprising, then, that
contemporary Christianity, prompted by a renewed interest and
research in liturgical worship, has accorded to this early period
a particular place and importance in its investigations. It is
against such a background that the present volume came to be
written, for no serious study of the early Western liturgy would
be complete without a comprehensive investigation and assessment of so vital a document as Verona lxxxv (80).

There are two or three small points which must be mentioned
at this stage. Both the terms 'Leonine' and 'Sacramentary' are
unsatisfactory in relation to this manuscript, since neither is in
any way an accurate description. A similar difficulty arises in
respect of what have come to be called the Gelasian and
Gregorian Sacramentaries. Whilst the term 'Sacramentary' is
allowable of these documents, I would find the same difficulty
in ascribing the description 'Gelasian' and 'Gregorian' to them
as I would in using the term 'Leonine' of the Verona manuscript. It would have been fussy to print these words in quotation marks throughout the book, but the reader is asked to
regard them as if they were so printed. So far as the Latin text
of the Verona lxxxv (80) is concerned, I have preserved faithfully the original as it is reproduced in Mohlberg's edition.
There has been no editing of the original text.

Most of what comprises this present volume was originally presented as a thesis for the degree of Doctor of Philosophy in the University of Oxford. I must acknowledge my grateful thanks to the late Dr. F. L. Cross for his untiring enthusiasm for this work, also for his advice and help at every stage of its preparation. Indeed it was he who first suggested that the thesis might be considered by the Oxford Theological Monographs Committee with a view to its being published. My thanks are also due to Dr. G. G. Willis, who read the typescript and suggested a number of improvements and additions at that stage; and to the Clarendon Press for their various helpful comments and observations in preparing this work for printing.

DAVID M. HOPE

Liverpool
April 1970

OXFORD THEOLOGICAL MONOGRAPHS

Oxford Theological Monographs

CANONS OF THE COUNCIL OF SARDICA
A.D. 343
A Landmark in the Early Development of Canon Law
By HAMILTON HESS. 1958

THE NEW TEMPLE
The Church in the New Testament
By R. J. MCKELVEY. 1968

NEW LITURGICAL FEASTS
IN LATER MEDIEVAL ENGLAND
By R. W. PFAFF. 1970

THE LEONINE
SACRAMENTARY

*A Reassessment of
its Nature and Purpose*

BY

D. M. HOPE

OXFORD UNIVERSITY PRESS

1971

Oxford University Press, Ely House, London W. 1

GLASGOW NEW YORK TORONTO MELBOURNE WELLINGTON
CAPE TOWN SALISBURY IBADAN NAIROBI DAR ES SALAAM LUSAKA ADDIS ABABA
BOMBAY CALCUTTA MADRAS KARACHI LAHORE DACCA
KUALA LUMPUR SINGAPORE HONG KONG TOKYO

PRINTED IN GREAT BRITAIN
AT THE UNIVERSITY PRESS, OXFORD
BY VIVIAN RIDLER
PRINTER TO THE UNIVERSITY

PREFACE

IN spite of the complexity of the subject, it is imperative in these days that, so far as is possible, the evolution and development of the Christian liturgy be appreciated and understood by the individual believer; for ultimately the liturgy is the means by which, and the framework within which, the Christian lives out his day-to-day existence. On the part of every Christian, therefore, one would expect some acquaintance with the historical and social aspects of liturgical change and development, and a rudimentary understanding of the principles of liturgical worship, against which contemporary movements might be informatively viewed. It has long been acknowledged that much of the early history and development of the Western liturgy is tenuous and obscure. It is perhaps surprising, then, that contemporary Christianity, prompted by a renewed interest and research in liturgical worship, has accorded to this early period a particular place and importance in its investigations. It is against such a background that the present volume came to be written, for no serious study of the early Western liturgy would be complete without a comprehensive investigation and assessment of so vital a document as Verona lxxxv (80).

There are two or three small points which must be mentioned at this stage. Both the terms 'Leonine' and 'Sacramentary' are unsatisfactory in relation to this manuscript, since neither is in any way an accurate description. A similar difficulty arises in respect of what have come to be called the Gelasian and Gregorian Sacramentaries. Whilst the term 'Sacramentary' is allowable of these documents, I would find the same difficulty in ascribing the description 'Gelasian' and 'Gregorian' to them as I would in using the term 'Leonine' of the Verona manuscript. It would have been fussy to print these words in quotation marks throughout the book, but the reader is asked to regard them as if they were so printed. So far as the Latin text of the Verona lxxxv (80) is concerned, I have preserved faithfully the original as it is reproduced in Mohlberg's edition. There has been no editing of the original text.

Most of what comprises this present volume was originally presented as a thesis for the degree of Doctor of Philosophy in the University of Oxford. I must acknowledge my grateful thanks to the late Dr. F. L. Cross for his untiring enthusiasm for this work, also for his advice and help at every stage of its preparation. Indeed it was he who first suggested that the thesis might be considered by the Oxford Theological Monographs Committee with a view to its being published. My thanks are also due to Dr. G. G. Willis, who read the typescript and suggested a number of improvements and additions at that stage; and to the Clarendon Press for their various helpful comments and observations in preparing this work for printing.

DAVID M. HOPE

Liverpool
April 1970

CONTENTS

ABBREVIATIONS

C.S.E.L.   Corpus Scriptorum Ecclesiasticorum Latinorum (Vienna 1866–).

D.A.C.L.   *Dictionnaire d'Archéologie Chrétienne et de Liturgie*, ed. F. Cabrol, O.S.B., and H. Leclercq, O.S.B. (15 vols., 1907–53).

Ephem. Lit.   *Ephemerides Liturgicae* (Rome, 1887–).

J.T.S.   *Journal of Theological Studies* (London, 1900–5; Oxford, 1906–49; N.S., Oxford, 1950–).

Lib. Pont.   *Le Liber Pontificalis*, ed. L. Duchesne (Bibliothèque des Écoles Françaises d'Athènes et de Rome, 2 vols., 1886–92).

P.L.   *Patrologia Latina*, ed. J. P. Migne (221 vols., Paris, 1844–64).

INTRODUCTION

T HE origins of the Christian Church in Verona, admittedly interwoven with a good deal of legend, are described in the eighth-century document known as the 'Carmen Pipinianum',[1] which, in addition to a description of the city and an enumeration of its churches, contains a list of the first eight bishops from St. Euprepius (possibly 3rd century) to St. Zeno (d. A.D. 380). The growth of Verona as a centre of Christian learning—indeed, the very existence of the city itself—must ultimately be attributed to one important factor, the city's position at the intersection of the chief lines of communication in Italy and southern Europe. Even during the Roman period the city was the meeting-place for the three great roads: the Augusta, the Gallica, and the Posthumia. In such a centre as this it is not surprising to find art and culture developing and each successive age leaving its imprint upon the city. Similarly, developments within the more specifically Christian sphere are reflected in the city—its art, worship, and architecture. It is upon the site of one of the ancient centres of Christian worship, possibly of the fifth century, that the present Cathedral now stands.

To this Cathedral is attached the famous Chapter Library of Verona, in which was discovered the codex lxxxv (80), the Leonine Sacramentary. During the last war much of Verona, both inhabitants and monuments of historical worth, suffered from widespread air attack and to this the buildings of the Chapter Library were no exception; they were almost completely destroyed. However, the present librarian, Monsignor Giuseppe Turrini, will recount to any visitor the long and laborious task of the work of reconstruction; the present state of the library is to be attributed almost wholly to the effort and zeal of

---

[1] Cf. L. A. Muratori, *Rerum Italicarum Scriptores* (Milan, 1723), vol. ii, pt. 2, p. 1095. The 'Carmen Pipinianum', or 'Veronae Rythmica Descriptio Antiqua' as it is described by Muratori, was written by King Pippin (d. A.D. 768). It was while he was in Verona that Pippin composed this poem, which describes, in a somewhat romantic fashion, the glories of the city. The eighth-century manuscript of the poem is among the collection of the Chapter Library. It was first edited by J. Mabillon in *Vetera Analecta* (Paris, 1675), vol. i, pp. 371–6.

Mgr. Turrini. The library, though of no great size, is of immense value; Lowe speaks of it as 'that queen of ecclesiastical collections'.[1] Almost all the oldest of the extant codices of the collection are entirely devoted to Christian letters. The other documents range over widely differing ecclesiastical topics—patristic, biblical, conciliar, and liturgical. Among the more famous and precious of its texts are the Virgil and Euclid of the sixth century, the 'Institutions of Gaius' of the sixth century, the 'Didascalia Apostolorum' of the fifth century (palimpsest), and the 'sacramentarium Wolfgangi' of the tenth century. In addition to these, there are preserved in the library a number of very rare and in some cases unique examples of old musical prints, and to these have been added a large collection of books printed before the nineteenth century, also the valuable library of the Academia Filarmonica which has now been deposited in the Chapter Library.

The impression gained by an examination of the collection as a whole is one of diversity rather than uniformity of type. The support for Traube's[2] suggestion that the old manuscripts to be found there were generally of local origin is rather scanty though the suggestion itself is reasonable enough and there is no strong evidence against it. There are some manuscripts which display characteristics so peculiar that similar texts are not to be found either in the remainder of the Verona collection or in the whole of Italy. But, as Lowe points out, the present collection doubtless represents different scriptoria.[3]

The history of the output of the Cathedral scriptorium is to a large extent reflected in the Verona codices still in the Chapter Library. However, a problem which has given rise to much debate in the past and still remains unsolved is that of the date at which such a scriptorium, native to Verona, came into being. It is quite certain that Ursicinus, lector of the Cathedral in the sixth century, wrote the codex xxxviii (36), containing the works of Sulpicius Severus. This codex is clearly dated A.D. 517 at Verona, and would appear to be the oldest of the whole collection.[4] Lowe is of the opinion that there was a scriptorium at

---

[1] E. A. Lowe, *Codices Latini Antiquiores*, vol. iv (Oxford, 1947), Introduction, p. xix.

[2] L. Traube, *Vorlesungen und Abhandlungen*, vol. i (Munich, 1909), pp. 47 ff.

[3] Lowe, op. cit., Introduction, p. xix.

[4] This codex contains the following insertion on fol. 117: 'Perscribtus codex hec

Verona by the sixth century and that the Sulpicius Severus codex provides clear evidence of such a fact. De Beer,[1] however, whilst allowing that the codex xxxviii (36) was written at Verona in A.D. 517, maintains that this stands alone among the manuscripts of that date in having been written at Verona. He considers that there is no evidence which would point to the existence of a native school of writing at Verona before the seventh century. He contends rather that the early Verona manuscripts have come to Verona from elsewhere. By the ninth century, however, the existence of a scriptorium in Verona is unquestioned. A considerable reorganization of the Cathedral Chapter and also of the library took place during that period, in the episcopate of Ratoldus, who placed the scriptorium in charge of his accomplished archdeacon, Pacificus.[2] It was during this period that Verona as a centre of sacred learning became influential and played an important role in the life of Western Christendom. The library certainly contains a number of codices which are of foreign origin and can be given a date earlier than that of Pacificus. However, in view of the reorganization plan which was effected by Ratoldus, and in addition to the publication of new books, others were acquired from foreign scriptoria and these undoubtedly influenced the work of the Verona scriptorium. Again, the great cultural and ecclesiastical atmosphere prevalent in Bobbio throughout the ninth and tenth centuries would certainly have been felt in Verona also; it is not surprising therefore that some of the products of that centre should have found their way to the Verona library.

As important a name as any in connection with the long history of the Verona library is that of the Marchese Francesco Scipio Maffei (1675–1755). A native of Verona, he was educated at a Jesuit college; his education was, however, interrupted for some time when he joined the ranks to fight in the war of the Spanish Succession. In 1711, a year after his release from the

(Verona) de vita beati martini epi. et conf. et beati pauli SS. sub die Kal. aug. agapito UC. C. ind. decimae per ursicinium lect. ecclesiae veronensis.' The same manuscript also shows signs of having been read at a later date by Pacificus, who made various transpositions and insertions in the text.

[1] R. De Beer, *Sitzungsberichte* of the Vienna Academy, philos.-hist. Classe, 1911, no. 11, pp. 89–90.

[2] In addition to his literary accomplishments he was also an architect and inventor. The project for the second basilica of St. Zeno and plans for other Veronese churches have been attributed to him.

forces, he visited Turin and acquainted himself with the collection of manuscripts at the Royal Library there. When he returned to Verona, having seen these listed on the epitaph of Pacificus, his sole aim was to know what had become of the manuscript treasures of the Cathedral and particularly those written under the said Pacificus.[1] These numbered approximately two hundred. But Canon Carinelli, the aged librarian of the time, professed no knowledge of the supposed books. Finally in October 1713 an old press or cupboard was opened in the dimly-lit muniment room, revealing only a number of inventories and deeds of various kinds. The top of the cupboard was merely covered with rough slats and, when these had been removed, the treasures were discovered. Maffei himself described the receptacle in which these were contained as 'being like the boot of a stage-coach'.

The Cathedral and its adjacent buildings, including the Chapter Library, being built very near the river Adige, are very vulnerable to flooding of the river; it is known that in 1575 a serious flood of the river Adige occurred which severely damaged parts of the Capitular buildings. Several of the manuscripts which were rediscovered had obviously suffered from the flood water during this time.[2] In 1624, when further alterations were made in the Cathedral, the library was taken over for use as a Chapter House and before the new library was erected the books were placed elsewhere and the manuscripts placed in this cupboard top so that if another flood did occur they were in no danger of water reaching them. During the year 1630, just when the building work was scheduled to begin, Verona was taken by the plague, which claimed many of the Cathedral officials; the Cathedral itself was, for a period of time, almost completely deserted. When the library was opened, some time later, the existence of the manuscripts had been forgotten; it is to the persistence of Maffei, in his determination to know what had become of the missing codices, that we must ultimately attribute the rediscovery of the manuscript containing the text of the Leonine Sacramentary.

[1] This epitaph, of the sixteenth century, is to be found in one of the chapels of the north aisle of the present Cathedral.

[2] Cf. C. H. Turner, 'An Arian Sermon from a ms. in the Chapter Library of Verona', *J.T.S.* 13 (1911–12), p. 19.

1

THE MANUSCRIPT

THE Verona codex which is our immediate concern is that which bears the class mark lxxxv (80) and is commonly designated the Leonine Sacramentary. The manuscript itself is incomplete. Though originally made up of twenty gatherings, with eight leaves each, and three additional leaves at the end, the present form of the manuscript consists of one hundred and thirty-nine leaves, each measuring *c.* 240 × 180 mm., with twenty-five long lines on each leaf. The leaves have been ruled on the flesh side; each bifolium has been ruled before folding. Single bounding lines enclose the actual text. An ancient device of pricking the parchment in order to guide the ruling is visible throughout much of the manuscript. The parchment itself has been well prepared, though the flesh sides appear rather rough; fortunately, however, these have retained the ink well and therefore remain legible. On the top of each page is a cross, under which the title of the month is written in uncial script between rather florid markings. Thus, for instance, the month of May will be displayed on fols. 16ᵛ and 17ʳ as '*f* mense *f*' (top of fol. 16ᵛ) and '*f* maio *f*' (top of fol. 17ʳ) and the month of June on fols. 22ᵛ and 23ʳ in a similar manner, thus: '*f* mense *f*' (top of fol. 22ᵛ) and '*f* iunio *f*' (top of fol. 23ʳ). Where the new month begins, except in the months of October and November, the title is announced in the space at the top of a new page; hence at the top of fol. 15ᵛ appears '*f* MENSE *f* MAIO *f*' in a brownish red colour, and on the opposite page (fol. 16ʳ), now in the normal brownish colour in which most of the text of the sacramentary is written, '*f* mense maio *f*'. Only four times in the whole manuscript does the word 'mense' not appear on the left-hand page—fols. 65ᵛ, 137ᵛ, 138ᵛ, and 139ᵛ. On fol. 40ʳ the new month of July begins; on the opposite side (fol. 39ᵛ) the word 'mense' is abbreviated to $\tilde{m}$; this occurs again on fol. 81ʳ, in the month of September. Abbreviations are used a number of times in these

titles which serve to indicate the months—fol. 81ʳ (*septemb*),
fol. 83ʳ (*sept*), fol. 101ʳ (*sem(t)*), fol. 105ʳ (*sep*), fol. 109ʳ (*seps*),
fol. 115ʳ (*octob*), fol. 120ʳ (*nob*), fol. 134ʳ (*dec*). At the beginning
of the manuscript the month of April is already in progress;
May begins on fol. 15ᵛ and ends on fol. 21ᵛ. On this folio only
22 lines are utilized, the rest of the page remaining empty; then
the month of June opens anew on fol. 22ʳ and ends on fol. 39ʳ.
July begins on fol. 39ᵛ and ends on fol. 65ᵛ; August opens on fol.
66ʳ and closes on fol. 80ʳ. The month of September opens on
fol. 80ᵛ and closes on fol. 114ᵛ. Thus so far each month has been
introduced with a fresh page. Indeed space is left empty at the
end of the month of May in order that June may open on the
next side. In the case of October and November, however, this
is not so. The last formulae of the month of September occupy
about 2/3 of the side of fol. 114ᵛ and on line 19 of that same side
the month of October is immediately begun. It closes on fol. 119ʳ
where again the same thing happens in the case of November.
The last formulae of October continue to about half-way down
the page. Again, the month of November is introduced on line
14 with the usual title. Whilst the script of these two titles is the
same as the others, and so too is the colouring (a rather brownish
red), they lack, in both cases, the usual flourishes, common to
the other titles, which occur at the head of the various folios to
indicate the months. The compiler seems to be quite erratic in
the way in which he sets out his material, since the last three
formulae of the month of November occupy only nineteen lines,
the remaining lines being empty. This is presumably so that he
can begin anew with the month of December on fol. 128ᵛ, which
is in fact what has happened. The cross at the top of each page
together with the titles which indicate the beginning of a new
month are all written in a brownish red colour.[1] Also in respect
of the titles of the various groups of Mass formulae it is true to
say that these too are generally written in this same colour, but
there are one or two notable exceptions to this. The title of the
new month, July, is to be found in red at the top of fol. 39ᵛ.
There then follows the long title VI IDUUM IULIARUM NATALE

[1] Cf. p. 23. The month of the civil year is not the only framework used in the
compilation of the Sacramentary. The separate groups, e.g. Ascension (IX) and
Pentecost (X), also form a convenient basis of arrangement for the material. Each
such group has a number attached to it, no doubt to preserve some order in the
material as a whole.

SCORUM MARTYRUM FELICIS PHILIPPI etc. in a brownish colour (the same as that in which the formulae of the book are written). However, the number of this particular group is in brownish red in the margin. In a similar way, though the title in the month of August appears in this brownish red colour at the top of fol. 66ʳ, the title of the first set of Mass formulae—IIII NON AUG N SCI STEFANI IN CYMETERIO CALLISTI VIA APPIA is again in the same ink as that of the rest of the text of the manuscript. The group number XVIIII is in the margin and is brownish red in colour. It seems to the present writer, after inspecting the manuscript, that it is highly likely that in the first place the Leonianum was written in the brownish ink throughout—including the titles of the months and the titles of the various sections. It is only after this that the compiler has gone over his work with the red colour. There are a number of titles which illustrate quite clearly that the red colour has been added over the brown—fol. 122ᵛ SANCTI SILVESTRI, fol. 73ʳ IN NATALE SANCTORUM FELICISSIMI ET AGAPITI. On fol. 122ᵛ in the title NATALE SANCTORUM CLEMENTIS ET FELICITATIS, which has clearly been brown to begin with and later worked over in red, the letter 'l' of Felicitas still remains in the original brown. There is evidence, however, that the compiler has, in some instances, had second thoughts and decided to add a title where formerly there was no title at all. On fol. 19ᵛ 'Praesumptio et Reparatio Primi Hominis', which shows no signs of having been previously written in brown ink, appears between lines 9 and 10, squeezed in between prayers 208 and 209, obviously to give some indication about the formula following; the words 'Post Infirmitate' appear in a similar fashion between lines 24 and 25 of fol. 32ʳ and clearly show that they were not written previously in brown ink. Again, the words IN PENTECOSTEN ASCENDENTIBUS A FONTE on fol. 18ᵛ have probably been added afterwards. They follow immediately after the formula 199 and go some way over into the right-hand-side margin. The title CONTRA INIMICOS CATHOLICAE PROFESSIONIS must be added to these examples. It follows immediately after the formula 217 of which the last line appears on line 9 of fol. 20ᵛ. The word PROFESSIONIS is written between lines 9 and 10. It is suggested that the title on fol. 59ʳ ORATIONES MATUTINAS VEL AD VESPERUM may have read originally ORATIONES MATUTINAS and the words VEL AD VESPERUM been added later. The words ORATIONES MATUTINAS have certainly been written in brown ink and then covered with red later, whereas the words VEL AD VESPERUM show no signs of having previously been written in brown.[1] By now it must be evident that only these two colours are employed by the compiler of our manuscript and as a whole the work shows no signs of particularly florid decoration or colour. On every occasion the numbers of the various groups are displayed in brownish red in the left-hand-side margin—XXV (fol. 119ʳ), XXXVIII (fol. 125ᵛ), together with the usual sign indicating a new group of Mass formulae.

A large number of abbreviations are used by the compiler throughout the text of the Sacramentary. The following will serve as examples: *b* 'bus', *q* 'que', *h* 'haec', *n* 'noster' and its cases, also *ni* 'nostri' and *ns* 'nostris', *omnp, omps, omp* 'omnipotens', *p* 'per', *sca* 'sanctus', *sci* 'sancti', *sce* 'sanctae, sancte', *sps, spiu, spm, spu* the various cases of 'spiritus'. In the several titles *N* is used as an abbreviation of 'natale'. The Divine Name 'Dominus' has a variety of abbreviations in its different cases—*dm, dni, dno, dnm, dne*; Christus is found in the forms *xps, xpo, xpm*. The opening formula of the proper preface never appears at all in the Leonianum in its entirety ('Vere dignum et iustum est, aequum et salutare, nos tibi semper et ubique gratias agere, domine, sancte pater, omnipotens aeterne deus . . .') but is simply reduced to its barest form, *V.D.* Similarly the formula at the end of any prayer, the words 'per dominum nostrum Iesum Christum filium tuum' (or in some cases 'per Christum dominum nostrum per quem te laudant angeli . . . sanctus . . .'), are contained within the one letter *p* at the end of the formula. Also a variety of endings attached to the proper prefaces is to be found in the Sacramentary—'propterea' (176, 273, 1270), 'propterea cum angelis' (15), 'et ideo' (177, 428), 'et ideo cum angelis' (2, 161, 823, 846, 1137), 'per hunc eundem' (179), 'offerimus et cetera' (202), 'unde cum angelis' (239, 244, 254), 'cum angelis' (29, 285), 'unde profusis gaudiis' (1245), 'unde profusis' (1247, 1250, 1262). The letter *m* is sometimes omitted and where this is so in the manuscript it is indicated by a line with a dot above, as in some Visigothic manuscripts; occasionally the line has a dot

---

[1] The note ITEM AD VESPERUM appears a little lower down on the same page as the fuller title ORATIONES MATUTINAS VEL AD VESPERUM, making the addition of VEL AD VESPERUM to the title ORATIONES MATUTINAS seem rather superfluous.

below as well as one above—'semper' *se÷per* (327), 'omnium *o÷nium,* 'omnibus' *o÷nibus* (251, 541, 816), 'etiam' *etia÷* (20), 'saevitiam' *saevitia÷* (29).

The dates upon which particular feasts are to be observed usually appear as part of the title to the particular group which they introduce: thus we find 'kal iul' (fol. 22ʳ), 'non aug' (fol. 66ʳ) 'idus aug' (fol. 70ʳ), 'prid kal oct' (fol. 82), 'prid kal dec' (fol. 128ᵛ). The punctuation is practically non-existent except for the occasional medial point. There are other points in the margins but Lowe considers it is more likely that some liturgical significance is indicated by them.

A later hand has added rubrics of varying kinds in the margins and corrections in the actual text; in some examples words have been erased altogether. The section entitled INCIPIUNT ORATIONES ET PRAECES DIURNAE affords numerous examples of the former (rubrics added by a later hand)—fol. 46ʳ ('contra lacerantes vel adulantes'; 'pro duplici corde'; 'orandum pro persequentibus'), fol. 47ᵛ ('in periculis vel prosperitate gratias referendas deo'), fol. 56ʳ ('humilibus adesse deum in cunctis operibus eorum'). As Mgr. Turrini put it, these introductory phrases, so to speak, are the product of someone who is anxious to compress the sometimes prolix nature of these proper prefaces into a short epigrammatic phrase. These marginal comments of an ascetical or doctrinal nature, which can also be seen on fols. 46ʳ, 47ᵛ, 54ᵛ, etc., are written in contemporary uncial and half-uncial script. Lowe goes on to suggest that these insertions are quite clearly out of place in a book which is designed for public or liturgical use;[1] but this is a point which is discussed more fully later.[2] On fols. 20ᵛ, 21ʳ, 33ᵛ, 44ᵛ, and 129ʳ a number of marginal notes occur, written in North Italian script, probably Veronese; it is cursive script and can be given a possible date in the eighth century. A similar type of cursive script can be seen in the other Verona manuscripts of the eighth century. The lower part of fol. 139ʳ and the whole of 139ᵛ contain a continuation of the liturgical text in different ink, by a seventh-century hand using mixed uncial and half-uncial script which has close similarities with other manuscripts found among the Verona collection.

A marginal note of interest and importance is to be found in

---

[1] Lowe, op. cit. iv, p. 32, no. 514.
[2] See below, p. 138.

the left-hand margin towards the top of the page of fol. 24ᵛ.
It reads as follows: 'In dei nomine Ratpert klerykus trudus
Egynoni.' The note is written in faint Greek characters. It makes
quite explicit references to Egino, Bishop of Verona (A.D. 772–
802) before Ratoldus; Ratpert (Robert) is obviously one of his
clergy. It is clear that this note establishes the connection between this codex and the city of Verona at least by the eighth
century—this is supported also by the evidence of other marginal comments. Apart from this no other mention is made
either in the marginal notes, or at the beginning, or at the end,
of names of those who might at some time have had connections
with the manuscript. At the bottom of this same page (fol. 24ᵛ)
following the formula 253 there is added the following formula
in a cursive hand: 'Preces populi tui, quaesumus Domine, cle-
menter adsume, ut nos servos tuos custodias ab omni malo adque
defendas'. The script is certainly North Italian and is of the
eighth century. The formula does not seem to appear elsewhere.

Many suggesions have been made concerning the meaning
and the import of the strange abbreviations to be found in the
margins and at the end of prayers in some cases, such as F E SP,
P SP FE and P E F SP, but since this is still a much-discussed point
and one which has produced a number of theories, a separate
section has been selected so that these can be dealt with independently.[1]

Mention must be made at this point of several rather dark
patches at certain places on the manuscript of the Leonianum;
though not greatly pronounced, these show obvious signs of
wear. I mentioned this point to Mgr. Turrini, who gave his
opinion that these dark patches were to be attributed to the
kissing of this book, as was the custom with the book of the
Gospels, as an act of veneration by the faithful.[2] But presumably
this would imply that the Leonianum was a Mass book for use
in public and that is where would receive such treatment.
However, in order to support his view Mgr. Turrini also remarked that Dom Mohlberg,[3] a close friend of his, had privately

---

[1] Cf. Appendix A, pp. 145–53.

[2] Against this it must be said that any kissing of the Missal at this period is highly
unlikely.

[3] This is a modification of a view expressed earlier. Cf. L. C. Mohlberg, O.S.B.:
'Io penso che la raccolta di preghiere di Verona non sia mai stata usata all'altare e
che nemmeno lo poteva essere' (*Ephem. Lit.* 1933, p. 4).

expressed the opinion to him that the Leonianum, the product of the Church, as it were, was also used at some stage as the liturgical book for a Christian community.

The script of the Leonianum is "an easy, informal uncial', which Lowe suggests is unusual in liturgical documents;[1] he therefore proposes that this copy was designed, not for use as a public Mass book but as a purely private collection. Clearly such a view clashes with that of Mgr. Turrini—but this is a subject which will be discussed more fully at a later stage.

In addition to the actual manuscript of the Leonine Sacramentary, a brief note must also be made of the Verona manuscript I (I) Appendix Fragm. I (fol. i–iii). This is written in uncial script of the sixth century and contains the following passages from the Old Testament: Ecclesiasticus 34:12–end, Proverbs 6:7–19, and Wisdom 10:10–11. 2. These three folios, each measuring c. 240 × 190 mm., are considerably damaged. Their origin is rather uncertain, but Lowe presumes they come from somewhere in Italy. The reason why this manuscript is mentioned at this point is that these leaves[2] once served as the flyleaves of Verona lxxxv (80), namely the Leonianum. The ninth-century notes on f. lv are in the hand of Pacificus, Archdeacon of Verona: 'R in men VII' and 'Admonitio ieiunii mensis VII Rq in men. VI. In qt XIIII. Invitatio plebis in ieiunio men decimi Rq in qt XV.' These obviously refer to the rubrics actually to be found in the fourteenth quire of the Sacramentary, as Maffei recognized.

The class-marking of the Verona manuscripts is arranged by a combination of the roman and of the arabic numerals. The system whereby the manuscripts were classified by Arabic numerals was that used before the codices were lost and it is likely that this is the work of the librarian Rezzano, who in the year 1625 compiled a catalogue of the manuscripts extant in that year. These class marks were to be found on the top right-hand corner of the first page and were in two series, one in red and the other in black. If it is assumed that 'lxxxv (80)' means 'lxxxv olim (80)' it is possible that a rearrangement of the classification numbers, by which this codex became 85 instead of 80, is the

---

[1] Lowe, op. cit. iv, p. 32, no. 514.
[2] The leaves were reassembled by Joannes Jacobus de Dionysiis, Canon of Verona, in 1758.

work of Dionisi, librarian, who in 1785 supplemented the earlier catalogue with a 'Paralipomena manuscriptorum codicum Capituli Veronensis'. No doubt the fresh discoveries were incorporated into the collection of existing manuscripts and the whole classification overhauled.

2

A HISTORY OF THE STUDY OF
THE MANUSCRIPT

I. Editions

IT is now over two hundred years ago since the codex lxxxv (80) of the Chapter Library of Verona was first published with notes. Giuseppe Bianchini[1] (1704–64), himself a native of Verona, is the first name which must be considered in this connection. Much of his life was actively devoted to scholarship —biblical, historical, and liturgical; his work was officially recognized both by Clement XII and by Benedict XIV—indeed the latter commissioned him to produce several works. Bianchini worked for many years at a large work on the text of Holy Scripture, *Vindiciae Canonicarum Scripturarum Vulgatae latinae editionis*, which was to be made up of several volumes, though in fact only the first, in which fragments of the 'Hexapla' are to be found, was actually published (Rome, 1740). However, of much greater importance in this field was his two-volume work, *Evangeliarium Quadruplex Latinae Versionis Antiquae* (Rome, 1749). But his *Demonstratio Historicae Ecclesiasticae Quadripartitae* (Rome, 1752–4) was his chief contribution to historical scholarship. Among his liturgical publications an outstanding study is that entitled *Liturgia antiqua hispanica, gothica, isidoriana, mozarabica, toletana mixta* (Rome, 1746), in which was printed a Mozarabic 'libellus orationum' which he had found in the Verona Library. An edition of an 'Ordo Romanus' was published in volume iii of the *Vita Romanorum Pontificum* of his uncle, Francesco Bianchini; again this edition was produced from a Verona manuscript. Giuseppe himself wrote the preface and his uncle added the notes. A collection of the texts of ancient sacramentaries had been planned by G. Bianchini but, being

---

[1] Cf. the Catholic Encyclopedia, vol. ii (London, 1947), p. 541; H. Hurter, S. J. *Nomenclator Litterarius* (Innsbruck, 1895), vol. iii, cols. 71–6.

absorbed in other more pressing studies, he could not find sufficient time for such a project.

The importance of the name of Giuseppe Bianchini, so far as
our present study is concerned, is in his publication, for the first
time, of the text of the Leonine Sacramentary.[1] Although Maffei
had actually discovered in the Chapter Library the Verona
manuscripts, it was Bianchini who produced the first printed
edition of this particular manuscript, lxxxv (80). The Leonine
Sacramentary was published in the fourth volume of his uncle's
edition (Rome, 1735)[2] of the *Vitae Romanorum Pontificum* of
Anastasius ('bibliothecarius'). The general title to the particular
items of this fourth volume is 'Prolegomena ad vitas Romanorum
pontificum Anastasio Bibliothecario attributas, auctore Josepho
Blanchino Veronensi Congregationis Oratorii de urbe presbyteri'. The actual text of the Sacramentary appears in Opus-
culum II on page xii and continues to page lvii. Following this
is the 'Index codicis Sacramentorum' on pages lviii–lx, which
records all proper names and titles in the Sacramentary together with the numbers which are attached to the titles. The
text of the Sacramentary is printed in double columns on each
page; comments and references to other liturgical books are
made in the extreme margins of each page alongside the text in
question. The less important titles such as 'post infirmitate',
'ad fontem', 'in dedicatione', etc., are not produced as part of
the text. They are noted in the margins, as are a number of the
marginal notes attached to some of the prefaces in the actual
manuscript. When referring to other liturgical books, Bianchini
mentions Tommasi's editions of the Missale Gothicum and the
Gregorian Sacramentary. For the latter, however, he also refers
to editions by Pamelius (1571) and Ménard (1642). Pamelius's
edition of the Ambrosian Missal is also mentioned. However,
Bianchini makes no note of parallel texts within the Sacramentary itself. Also, there is no indication that the last section
of the text does not really belong to the Sacramentary. Though
somewhat reduced in size, there is on page xxi of this first printed

[1] The first edition appeared under this title: 'Codex Sacramentorum vetus
Romanae Ecclesiae a Sancto Leone Papa I confectus. Primum prodit ex manu-
scripto libro numeralis notae XLI ante mille annos conscripto, qui exstat in Biblio-
theca eiusdem amplissimi Capituli Veronensis.'

[2] None of these four volumes is in the Bodleian Library, Oxford. They are
easily accessible, however, in the British Museum.

edition of the Sacramentary a reproduction of one of the pages of the actual manuscript (fol. 28ᵛ, that which contains the opening prayers of group XV 'In n apostolorum Petri et Pauli'). Undoubtedly it was Bianchini's text which was the best and most reliable until that produced by Feltoe many years later; certainly the designation 'Leonine', which has been associated for so long with the Sacramentary, is to be attributed to Bianchini.

The next scholar to be considered is Luigi Antonio Muratori (1672–1750),[1] who, although he was brought up in a relatively poor family in the district of Modena, became one of the chief scholars of the early eighteenth century.[2] Under the influence of Count Charles Borromeo the first work he undertook was at the Ambrosiana, Milan, where he collected together and edited ancient writings of various kinds. This resulted in his first publication in two volumes, *Anecdota Latina ex Ambrosianae Bibliothecae codicibus* (Milan, 1697–8), to which a further two volumes were added later (Padua, 1713). In 1700 he was appointed archivist and librarian in Modena, a position which he held until his death in 1750. One outstanding publication is his collection of ancient inscriptions, in four volumes, *Novus thesaurus veterum inscriptionum* (Milan, 1739–42), which enumerates in the fourth volume the ancient Christian inscriptions. More pertinent to our present task is his edition of various sacramentaries entitled *Liturgia Romana Vetus*.[3] Having received from Bianchini various notes preparatory to such a work, Muratori was already well equipped for the preparation of such a collection. The work is prefaced by a discussion of the early liturgy, both Eastern and Western, and a comparative study of the two. Although his work was based on the three 'Roman' sacramentaries—Leonine, Gelasian, and Gregorian—Muratori did incorporate into this edition the three sacramentaries of 'Gallican' origin which had previously been edited by Tommasi, namely the Gothicum, Francorum, and Gallicanum, together with the two 'Ordines Romani' edited by Mabillon. A general section entitled 'De Origine Sacrae Liturgiae' precedes his editions of the Leonine and Gelasian

---

[1] Cf. *D.A.C.L.* cxxviii–cxxix, cols. 536–43; Hurter, op. cit., vol. ii, cols. 1403–21.

[2] Cf. E. Bishop, *Liturgica Historica* (Oxford, 1918), p. 75, who endorses an opinion, already expressed, that Muratori was for Italy a Congregation of St. Maur in himself.   [3] Published in two volumes, Venice, 1748.

Sacramentaries in *Liturgia Romana Vetus*. Within this section the two chapters III and IV, entitled 'De Sacramentario Leoniano' and 'De festis in Leoniano' respectively, illustrate most clearly Muratori's own views on the material in the Sacramentary. His actual edition of the text extends from col. 293 to col. 484 and is printed in two columns on each page. Parallels with the manuscripts Vat. Reg. 337 and Vat. Ottob. 313 are noted; reference is also made to the Missale Gothicum (Tommasi's edition). Parallel texts within the Sacramentary itself are also noted, as are a number of the marginal notes (particularly those attached to the July prefaces). For his references to other liturgical documents Muratori has relied upon the editions produced by Tommasi, particularly those within his *Codices Sacramentorum Nongentis Annis Vetustiores* (1680) and *Antiqui Libri Missarum Romanae Ecclesiae* (1691). The part of the text on fol. 139[v] of the manuscript, which has obviously been added in a later hand, Muratori takes to be part of the official Sacramentary. For the most part, he merely reproduced the text from Bianchini;[1] it is very doubtful whether he ever consulted the original manuscript. However, he did add to Bianchini's text his own set of notes, but unfortunately he made a number of rather arbitrary alterations and emendations which have in fact rendered the text less valuable than that of Bianchini. Similarly his text of the Gregorian Sacramentary was totally inadequate. Although he had never actually consulted the two manuscripts, he attempted a fusion of Vat. Reg. 337 and Vat. Ottob. 313 into one whole work, which he named the Gregorian Sacramentary.[2]

---

[1] This edition was entitled 'Sacramentarium Leonianum sive Liber Sacramentorum Romanae Ecclesiae a sancto Leone papa I, ut videtur, confectus'.

[2] His method of dealing with the text of the two manuscripts caused considerable confusion and dislocation. He transferred a considerable part of the contents of the 'Gregorianum' to a position after the numbered sections of the supplement; thus cols. 241–72 of Muratori's text should have followed immediately after col. 138. Similarly another section of the 'Gregorianum' was transferred to a place between the proper prefaces (from Vat. Reg. 337) and the Benedictions (from Vat. Ottob. 313). The compiler's preface was printed in a footnote in col. 272 which, in this position, with part of the text already displaced, made references in the preface to other parts of the book completely unintelligible. The result of such a mixture of manuscripts has been the source of much confusion in the past in regard to the text of the Gregorian Sacramentary. Similarly in his edition of *Liturgia Romana Vetus* the Gregorian Vat. Reg. 337 is cited as Vat. Reg. 335. Because of this error in the number of the manuscript, it was for a long period of time given up as lost. Such an

The debt of the Western Church to the four Assemani[1] brothers is immense; for it was through their researches, collection of manuscripts, and publications that Syriac studies, and in general the history, hagiography, liturgy, and literature of the Oriental Church were first introduced into Europe during the eighteenth century. Joseph Aloysius Assemani (1710–82), having first been professor of Syriac at the Sapienza in Rome, was afterwards promoted professor of liturgy by Benedict XIV, who made him a member of the newly founded academy for historical research. A considerable contribution to the study of liturgy (and especially to the study of the Eastern liturgies) is to be found in his *Codex Liturgicus Ecclesiae Universae*, which is made up of thirteen volumes. Although the 'Codex' was unfortunately never completed, it is a work of outstanding skill and care; and though the text of some of the oriental liturgies is often incomplete and doubtful, these comparatively minor shortcomings in so massive a publication can perhaps be overlooked. The Leonine Sacramentary appears in the sixth volume of this 'Codex' and is simply a reproduction of Muratori's text with a short preface by Assemani. It appears third in a set of four sacramentaries: (i) Missale Romanorum Vetus (Gelasian), (ii) Missale Hierosolymitarum, (iii) Sacramentarium Veronense vulgo Leonianum, (iv) Missale Alexandrinum. It is to be noted that this is the first time the designation 'Sacramentarium Veronense' is used of the Sacramentary hitherto called 'Leonine'. No doubt this was an astute move on the part of Assemani during the debate on authorship.

Two celebrated brothers, natives of Verona, were the next to produce an edition of the Leonine Sacramentary. Both Girolamo (1702–81) and Pietro (1698–1769) Ballerini[2] were famous as theologians and canonists. The exceptional literary activity of the two brothers, especially that of Pietro in his dispute with the Absolute Probabilists, made their names famous throughout Italy. The attention of Pope Benedict XIV was drawn to their outstanding scholarship, and he commissioned them to prepare an edition of Pope Leo's works in refutation of the defective

edition, therefore, is of very little use at the present time. Cf. E. Bishop, op. cit.. note on p. 75, also his note in A. B. De Kuypers, *Book of Cerne* (1902), pp. 234–40.

[1] Cf. *D.A.C.L.* xi, cols. 2978–9; Hurter, op. cit., vol. iii, cols. 481–3.
[2] Hurter, op. cit., vol. iii, cols. 93–8; *Dictionnaire de théologie catholique*, ii (1905), cols. 131–2.

edition published by Quesnel. Quesnel had produced a scholarly edition of all the writings of Pope Leo; however, this was almost immediately placed on the Index because of heretical opinions expressed in the notes accompanying his text. In order to produce a new and revised edition of the works of Leo, the two Ballerini were given free access to all the libraries in Rome for a period of almost nine years in length. The edition *Sancti Leonis Magni Romani Pontificis Opera*[1] was published in three volumes and contained an elaborate refutation of and additions to the work of Quesnel. The third volume is a penetrating study of the sources of Canon Law. Quesnel had published a collection of canons which he considered to have been in use under Popes Innocent I, Zosimus, and Leo I. In addition to disproving this, the Ballerini produced, in an improved version, earlier Latin editions of the canons, together with some very old, hitherto unknown, versions of Greek canons. As in the case of Muratori, it is doubtful whether the Ballerini consulted the original manuscript at Verona for their edition of the Leonine Sacramentary. If they did consult it, they cannot have made a thorough examination of the text; and like Muratori they introduced a number of emendations and additions of their own throughout. For the most part, however, their text is basically that of Bianchini.

It was this edition of Leo's works that Migne (1800–75) reproduced in his *Patrologia Latina*[2] (vols. 54–6), the edition of the Leonine Sacramentary being contained in volume 55. (Feltoe adds, in this context, 'with fewer misprints than usual'.) The notes which accompany the Ballerini text in Migne are those which first appeared with Muratori's text in his *Liturgia Romana Vetus*.

Thus it is quite clear that of all the editions noted above the first (Bianchini's) is by far the most accurate and valuable. Feltoe remarks: 'Except for the comparative rarity and positive bulki-

---

[1] Rome, 1753–7. The Sacramentary was published in the second volume of this work in 1756 (pp. 1–160) under the title 'Liber Sacramentorum Romanae Ecclesiae omnium vetustissimus, e millenario codice Capituli Veronensis editus, et Leoni Magno in vulgatis adscriptus, non pauca continens quae eundem pontificem habent auctorem'.

[2] The complete work of the Ballerini had the following title: 'Sancti Leonis Magni, Romani pontificis, opera omnia, post Paschasii Quesnelli recensionem ad complures et praestantissimos mss. codices ab illo non consultos exacta, emendata, et ineditis aucta: praefationibus, admonitionibus et annotationibus illustrata curantibus Petro et Hieronymo fratribus Balleriniis, presbyteris Veronensibus.'

ness of the book there would be little need to reprint the text now.' Later editions have consisted of reproductions of Bianchini's, for the most part, together with emendations in the text and notes added by the particular editor.

Feltoe relates how his own edition *Sacramentarium Leonianum* (Cambridge, 1896) was the result of work done during the course of two autumnal visits to Verona in 1894 and 1895. We learn that, whilst Feltoe had consulted earlier editions of the text, he had also closely examined the manuscript in Verona; undoubtedly this was the first occasion that the manuscript had been carefully consulted or even consulted at all since its publication by Bianchini. Feltoe's edition incorporated a useful short introduction and a set of notes on the text; at the time it was by far the best and most handy edition; it had also corrected many errors of former editions. However, in spite of this, his edition still contained a number of inaccuracies and was also without important palaeographical notes.

In 1956, however, as the first volume in the series 'Rerum Ecclesiasticarum Documenta' (Series Maior: Fontes I) under the editorship of Dom L. C. Mohberg (1878–1963),[1] the title *Sacramentarium Veronense* appeared. Again the Verona manuscript has been carefully examined and a completely new text produced; variant readings and suggested emendations form part of the critical apparatus at the foot of each page. Important parallels with the sacramentaries of the Gelasian and Gregorian type are noted there also. Without doubt one of the most important features of this production is the very full and informative introduction. This not only contains an exhaustive bibliography together with sections on date and authorship, but also important palaeographical material lacking in the former editions. Following the actual text of the Verona manuscript other allied documents are printed;[2] the edition also contains a useful concordance.[3] This latest edition of the text is certainly a vast improvement upon earlier editions and may be regarded as

[1] For an appreciation of his work and also a bibliography cf. B. Neunheuser, 'In memoriam L. Cuniberti Mohlberg, O.S.B.', *Ephem. Lit.* 78 (1964), pp. 58–62.

[2] The texts of the Ravenna Rotulus, the fragment of a 'libellus' (Milan, Ambrosiana O 210), the Phillipps fragment cod. 105 (Phillipps 1667) Berlin.

[3] Cf. P. Bruylants, *Concordance verbale du sacramentaire léonien* (Extrait de l'Archivum Latinitatis Medii Aevi, 18 [1945], pp. 51–376 and 19 [1948], pp. 39–405), Louvain, 1948.

definitive. Not least valuable is the edition's scheme of numbering each formula as it occurs in the text, which makes reference to any such formula much more convenient than it had been hitherto.

II. Studies

Many outstanding names are connected with the study of the Leonianum; a short survey of the contributions of the most important of these must now follow.

It was in the very first edition of G. Bianchini that the name 'Leonine' became attached to the Sacramentary; this was the result of his recognizing parallels between sections of the Sacramentary and certain passages in the writings of Pope Leo. It was upon this point, namely the authorship of the Sacramentary, that much debate was, and still is, centred. J. A. Orsi[1] (1692–1761) in a letter to Bianchini expressed the opinion that the work was solely that of Gelasius. However, Eusebius Amort (1692–1775), also writing to Bianchini, stated that he did not consider either Gelasius or Leo to be the author of the Sacramentary; he wrote:

non est opus unius alicuius pontificis, sed est Sacramentarium Romanorum Pontificum, usu receptum primis temporibus, auctum tamen et interpolatum per varios pontifices usque ad tempora Gelasii papae. Specialiter in hoc sacramentario agnoscuntur manus Sixti III, Leonis I, et Felicis III.[1]

Although Muratori in his *Liturgia Romana Vetus* considered the Sacramentary reflected the age of Felix III (483–92 A.D.), he did not ascribe its actual authorship to that Pope. In this same work he expresses the following opinion:

egregium sane ac pretiosum venerandae antiquitatis monumentum, cui par in hoc genere non reperias, utpote quod in eo exhibeatur omnium vetustissima liturgia, quae Romae olim in usu fuit. Dolendum tantum modo quod non integrum opus ad nos pervenerit, cum multa exciderint, et praesertim orationes pro compluribus dominicis diebus.

[1] Migne, *P.L.* 55, Preface, p. 1.

In addition to that produced by Bianchini, the editions of Muratori and the Ballerini also contained a set of notes on points of interest in the text. Thus, throughout the whole of the seventeenth and eighteenth centuries, the results of various studies on the Sacramentary were to be found only in the prefaces and notes alongside the text as published by successive editors. Undoubtedly the main topic of discussion centred upon the authorship of the Sacramentary and therefore, by implication, upon the date of its composition also. Hardly any opinions were expressed concerning the date of the manuscript itself; we do, however, know of one opinion which placed the codex at the end of the eighth century or the beginning of the ninth.[1]

It was with the publication of his book *Origines du culte chrétien* (1889) that L. Duchesne[2] (1843–1922) brought into prominence the view that the Leonianum was only a private collection, drawn up and arranged with a minimum of intelligence. The contents within a number of proper prefaces belonging to the July group XVIII convinced him that he could not uphold the traditional view that the Leonianum was the first of an official series of sacramentaries put out by Rome. He writes: 'this manner of putting one's adversaries in the pillory, or worse than the pillory, is clearly foreign to the recognized methods of the Roman Church.' Again Duchesne raises the question of the dating of the collection and it is he who puts forward the suggestion that several of the references to war in the prayers of group XVIII are to be viewed in the context of the siege of Rome in A.D. 537–8 by Vitiges. Thus it is Duchesne, an eminent scholar in the field of early Church history and archaeology, who for the first time makes a break with the more conservative theories regarding the nature of the Leonine Sacramentary.

Ferdinand Probst[3] directed his great erudition and careful scholarship to a study of liturgy and in particular to the field of early liturgy. No doubt he is chiefly remembered for his

---

[1] Cf. Hurter, op. cit., vol. iii, cols. 71–6. Bayerus had expressed this opinion in his historical work 'De Damaso et Laurentio' (Rome, 1756).

[2] L. Duchesne, *Origines du culte chrétien* (Paris, 1889); Eng. trans. by M. L. McClure under the title *Christian Worship* (London, 1903).

[3] Cf. *D.A.C.L.* ix, cols. 1731–2; xiv, cols. 1887–9. Probst's chief contributions are to be found in two works: *Die ältesten römischen Sakramentarien und Ordines* (Münster, 1892); 'Duchesne, "Über die drei ältesten römischen Sakramentarien"', *Zeitschrift für katholische Theologie*, 15 (1891), pp. 198–213.

conservatism, that is, his defence of the view that the eighth book of the Apostolic Constitutions was the universal liturgy of the Church from the earliest times. The value of his work lay chiefly in his careful and assiduous study of patristic and liturgical texts.

Although it is true that his conclusions may be regarded as very traditional, at the same time much of his discussion was based on the most vague allusions in any particular text and tended to be rather speculative, thus destroying much of the value of his scholarship.[1] For Probst, as for many commentators on the Leonianum, the very disorder of the manuscript was an interesting and important feature. Although he attributes material in the Sacramentary to Leo (d. A.D. 461) and Damasus (d. A.D. 384), for the most part he gives the compilation (as a whole) a date about the fifth century and rejects the opinion of Duchesne,[2] who suggests the sixth century as being most appropriate. Probst supposes that the compiler of the Leonianum has collected together a number of 'libelli missarum', which had previously existed independently. These 'libelli', he maintains, formed an intermediate stage between the period when the liturgy was always celebrated along the same lines, as exemplified in primitive times, and the age of the sacramentaries. The compilation of the Leonianum is, as it were, the first step in this direction. He observed that the material within the Sacramentary was not arranged primarily with the liturgical year in mind, as it was in the Gelasian and Gregorian Sacramentaries; the months of the civil year form the dominant feature of arrangement. It would be true to say that Probst, whilst his studies on the Leonianum bring forward new suggestions, never completely followed up the historical arguments regarding the 'libelli missae' and, as we have already observed about much of his work, he found it difficult to free himself from conservative attitudes and viewpoints.

Feltoe[3] considers the Sacramentary to be a very imperfect collection of Mass formulae, destined to be recopied at a later date. The manuscript of codex lxxxv of Verona is the original and is unique—he gives the collection about the same date as the manuscript, i.e. about the seventh century. The essential

[1] Leclercq remarks about Probst's own work: 'Plus de conscience que de talent, plus de talent que de goût, point d'art.'
[2] L. Duchesne, op. cit., pp. 137–9.
[3] C. L. Feltoe, *Sacramentarium Leonianum* (Cambridge, 1896), Introduction, p. xv.

feature of the work of both Feltoe and Lejay[1] is that they recognize the ancient character of certain of the prefaces. Lejay certainly allows that some of the prefaces have connections with events in the pontificate of Damasus, whilst the solution he suggests to the question raised by much of the polemical material in some of the prefaces is that this reflects the quarrels between clergy and monks which occurred during the seventh century. A. Dufourcq,[2] on the other hand, in his dissertation concerning Manichaeism among the Latin peoples, is in an incidental way occupied with the Leonianum and chiefly with the polemical passages. He is content to fix the date of composition about the time of Gelasius (A.D. 492–6) or of Symmachus (A.D. 498–514). Also he is careful to point out the Roman origin of the Sacramentary.

The studies of Buchwald[3] on the Leonianum led him to suggest that the author was St. Gregory of Tours. Though E. Rank[4] had already proposed this hypothesis, without, however, attaching much importance to it, Buchwald took it up and developed it. He considered the Leonianum was preparatory to and a basis for the Gelasian Sacramentary. This hypothesis, not surprisingly, has been contested and it can be said that such a view is virtually impossible. However, on other points (e.g. the explanation of the signs F E SP etc. and the preface 'de falsis fratribus') the results at which he has arrived must be given due consideration.

Passing reference must be made to the work of Martin Rule[5] on the text of the Sacramentary. He produces three successive hypotheses that the text is the result of redactions from three popes, Leo, Hilary, Simplicius. This sterile, artificial, stichometrical approach to the text can only end in disaster; the

[1] P. Lejay, 'Le sacramentaire véronais, chronique de littérature chrétienne', *Revue d'histoire et de littérature religieuses*, 2, (1897), pp. 190–2.

[2] A. Dufourcq, *De Manichaeismo apud latinos quinto sextoque saeculo atque de latinis apocryphis libris* (Paris, 1900), pp. 14–15.

[3] R. Buchwald, 'Das sogenannte Sacramentarium Leonianum und sein Verhältnis zu den beiden andern römischen Sakramentarien', *Weidenauer Studien*, 2 (1908), pp. 185–251.

[4] E. Ranke, *Das kirchliche Perikopsystem* (Berlin, 1847), pp. 109–14. Note also the indebtedness of Edmund Wilson to this work for a revival of interest in the Preface (Hucusque) to the supplement of the 'Hadrianum'. E. Bishop, op. cit., p. 347.

[5] M. Rule, 'The Leonine Sacramentary: an analytical study', *J.T.S.* 9 (1908), pp. 515–56; 10 (1909), pp. 54–99.

conclusions of Rule's work are highly speculative and question-able. They are better disregarded.

Lietzmann,[1] in more recent times, was the scholar who gave new impetus to the whole problem of dating the contents of the codex. Since then several major contributions have appeared. Dom B. Capelle,[2] on the grounds of style and language, con-cluded that at least two sets of Mass prayers were to be ascribed to Pope Gelasius. He cites examples of peculiarities of style in the Gelasian writings and finds parallels to these in two sets of prayers in the Leonianum.[3] If Capelle's conclusions are accepted, then it is quite clear that, on the evidence presented, many more sets of formulae exhibit similar characteristics, and are there-fore to be attributed to Gelasius also. Indeed both Callwaert[4] and Coebergh[5] considered the greater part of the prayers and prefaces to have been the work of Gelasius, who, though his pontificate was short, had probably produced much literary work under the two preceding popes.

The study of Emmanuel Bourque[6] is prefaced by a useful list of editions, bibliography, and manuscripts allied to the Leo-nianum. A brief study is made of each group of Mass prayers, attempting, so far as is possible, to suggest the occasion and place of composition and consequently a date also. Of necessity many of the dates which Bourque suggests are indefinite, but this is not surprising in view of the difficulties presented by the text, which on so many occasions makes definite dating an impossi-bility. Most of the groups of formulae he attributes to a period later than A.D. 400, and more than half he ascribes to a date after A.D. 500. On the supposition that the place of origin of the material within the Leonianum is Rome, Bourque proceeds to distinguish between those formulae which are of papal origin and

---

[1] H. Lietzmann, 'Petrus und Paulus in Rom', *Arbeiten zur Kirchengeschichte*, 1 (ed. 2, 1927); idem, 'Zur Datierung des Sacramentarium Leonianum', *Jahrbuch für Liturgiewissenschaft*, 2 (1922), pp. 101–2. Lietzmann's views on the dating of the group 'In natale episcoporum' are perhaps the most important so far as our present study is concerned.

[2] B. Capelle, 'Messes du pape S. Gélase dans le sacramentaire léonien', *Revue bénédictine*, 65 (1945–6), pp. 12–41.

[3] See below, pp. 111 ff.

[4] C. Callewaert, 'S. Léon le Grand et les textes du léonien', *Sacris Erudiri*, 1 (1948), pp. 36–164.

[5] C. Coebergh, O.S.B., 'S. Gélase I, auteur principal du soi-disant sacramen-taire léonien', *Ephem. Lit.* 64 (1950), pp. 214–37 and 65 (1951), pp. 171–81.

[6] E. Bourque, *Étude sur les sacramentaires romains*, vol. i (Rome, 1948), pp. 63–169.

those which have their origin in the city of Rome itself or one of the suburban cemeteries just outside the city centre. Like Probst before him, Bourque considers that the compiler must have collected together a number of hitherto independent 'libelli missarum'; these he selected from some central place in Rome itself where such material would be easily accessible. Unfortunately Bourque's study is lacking in important palaeographical material and information on the actual manuscript itself. However, whilst regarding the Verona manuscript as a 'unicum' he assigns it to the early part of the seventh century.

A further important study of the sources of the Leonine Sacramentary is made by A. Stuiber.[1] His chief aim is to show that the Leonianum is not a sacramentary in the accepted sense of the word but rather a collection of 'libelli missarum', made privately and circulated independently. He makes a brief analysis of each part of the text and assesses the content with regard to authorship and date. Particular references to the city of Rome are collected together; it is these which are taken to indicate the Roman origin of much of the material. Thus the material which comprises the Leonianum he considers to have been taken from three distinct sources: (i) the liturgical collection of the papal archives, (ii) the 'libelli sacramentorum' of a Roman presbyter, (iii) a number of similar 'libelli' already attached to an existing Roman Calendar.

Antoine Chavasse,[2] after having made a study of the historical references in the Sacramentary, has been led to ascribe much of the material within the book to Pope Vigilius (A.D. 537–55). He holds that about sixty series of Mass formulae were probably composed within the years A.D. 537 and 538, i.e. during and immediately after the siege of Rome by the Ostrogoths under Vitiges. Chavasse makes a careful comparison of the historical references within the text of the Sacramentary and the account of the events in the Gothic wars related by Procopius of Caesarea. Procopius himself had been appointed secretary to Belisarius and had accompanied him in his campaigns against the Vandals and Ostrogoths; his accounts of these campaigns are both detailed and reliable. It is at some period

---

[1] A. Stuiber, 'Libelli Sacramentorum Romani', *Theophaneia*, 6 (Bonn, 1950).

[2] A. Chavasse, 'Messes du pape Vigile dans le sacramentaire léonien', *Ephem. Lit.* 64 (1950), pp. 161–213 and 66 (1952), pp. 145–219.

during the pontificate of Pelagius I (A.D. 556–61) that Chavasse considers the Gelasian sets of formulae to have been incorporated into the collection.

Among palaeographic studies the work of E. A. Lowe[1] must be mentioned. He describes the chief features of the codex, noting especially its script and marginal notes. Though the origin of the manuscript still remains uncertain and is the subject of much discussion, Lowe suggests Verona as the place where it was written. Since the codex was found at Verona, where it is known to have been for many years, and since it contains no features which clearly suggest any other centre, the conclusion is (though this is by no means proved) that it was produced there. On the other hand Dr. Rudolph De Beer,[2] who made a study of the manuscripts of Verona, concludes that Verona is not the home of this manuscript. He maintains, contrary to Lowe, that there was no scriptorium in Verona until the eighth century; however, in view of the paucity of evidence, this is a point upon which debate still continues.

Brief reference may be made to the two facsimile editions. The first was published by A. Dold and M. Wölfle under the title *Sacramentarium Leonianum*;[3] but the reproduction is somewhat reduced from the size of the actual manuscript, while on several pages the script is rather indistinct. Undoubtedly the better of the two is that published by F. Sauer, again under the title *Sacramentarium Leonianum*.[4] The script, marginal notes, and the brown and red colouring of the script are all very clearly reproduced, as is the general browny-yellow of the parchment itself. The exact size of the folios of the original manuscript is preserved.

[1] E. A. Lowe, *Codices Latini Antiquiores*, iv (Oxford, 1947), no. 514.

[2] R. De Beer, *Sitzungsberichte* of the Vienna Academy, Philos.-hist. Classe, 1911, no. 11, pp. 89–90.

[3] A. Dold and M. Wölfle, *Sacramentarium Leonianum* (Beuron, 1957).

[4] F. Sauer, *Sacramentarium Leonianum* (Codices selecti phototypice impressi, vol. i, Graz, 1960).

3

THE CONTENTS OF THE SACRAMENTARY

THE Leonine Sacramentary comprises a collection of a large number of sets of Mass prayers or formulae. The total number of formulae in the part of the manuscript which we now have is 1331, and these are divided into something like 300 sets,[1] thus giving an average of three to four formulae for each set. In any particular Mass, it is likely that the following items will occur: a collect (sometimes a second collect), an offertory prayer, a proper preface, a post-communion (sometimes also an 'oratio super populum'). The method of arrangement which is most noticeable at a first glance at the Sacramentary is the division of the material into months throughout the calendar year. The book, as we have it, opens in the month of April and continues to December. As the first three months and part of the fourth are missing, the original number of formulae remains unknown. Our manuscript, however, retains about three-quarters of the complete work in its original form. In addition to the comprehensive framework by the month, there is superimposed a further framework, a division into groups being thus created. The 300 or so sets of Mass formulae were once further subdivided into a total of forty-three groups for the whole year. The present text gives us thirty-five complete groups and one incomplete (the opening Mass). Each of the groups is numbered and has a title which indicates the contents of the sets of formulae following; thus the group for the feast of St. John Baptist has the number XIII, the group for the feast of SS. John and Paul XIV, SS. Peter and Paul XV; the numbers continue in a similar way to XLIII (the December Ember Masses), with which the Sacramentary closes. The result of the combination

---

[1] There are in fact 291 separate sections of formulae, but not all these may be termed 'sets'. Often such sections contain but one or two formulae, e.g. 380, 381; 176. Again, it is clear that many sections contain more than one 'set' of formulae.

of these two methods of arrangement may be seen in the table below. There are, however, occasions when the compiler has placed sets of formulae in the wrong group, but this particular feature is dealt with in the account below when the problem arises.

APRIL

| Group | VIII | (Mass sets i–v missing) Part of set vi to set xliii; sets of formulae for a feast of Martyrs |

MAY

Group	IX	Ascension (7 sets)
Group	X	Vigil of Pentecost (6 sets)
Group	XI	Pentecost (3 sets)
Group	XII	Ember Mass (1 set)

JUNE

Group	XIII	St. John Baptist (5 sets)
Group	XIV	SS. John and Paul (8 sets)
Group	XV	SS. Peter and Paul (28 sets)
Group	XVI	(Prayer for the consecration of virgins)

JULY

| Group | XVII | The Seven Brothers (9 sets) |
| Group | XVIII | 'Orationes et preaces diurnae' (45 sets) |

AUGUST

Group	XIX	St. Stephen, pope (9 sets for St. Stephen, protomartyr)
Group	XX	SS. Sixtus, Felicissimus, and Agapetus (8 sets)
Group	XXI	St. Laurence (14 sets)
Group	XXII	SS. Hippolytus and Pontianus (1 set for St. Hippolytus, 1 set for St. Agapetus)
Group	XXIII	SS. Adauctus and Felix (6 sets and 1 preface of the Apostles)

SEPTEMBER

Group	XXIV	SS. Cornelius and Cyprian (2 sets)
Group	XXV	St. Euphemia (3 sets)
Group	XXVI	Dedication of the Basilica of St. Michael (5 sets)

Group	XXVII	Ember Masses and other Masses (15 sets)
Group	XXVIII	Ordination prayers for bishops, deacons, and priests
Group	XXIX	Episcopal anniversary and other Masses (23 sets)
Group	XXX	Prayer for the consecration of virgins
Group	XXXI	Prayer for the 'velatio nuptialis'

OCTOBER

Group	XXXII	'De Siccitate Temporis' (6 sets)
Group	XXXIII	Requiem Masses (5 sets)
Group	XXXIV	St. Sylvester (3 formulae, of which one is for Pope Simplicius)

NOVEMBER

Group	XXXV	The Quattro Coronati (2 sets)
Group	XXXVI	St. Cecilia (5 sets)
Group	XXXVII	SS. Clement and Felicity (7 sets)
Group	XXXVIII	SS. Chrysogonus and Gregory, martyrs (1 set)
Group	XXXIX	St. Andrew (4 sets)

DECEMBER

Group	XL	Christmas (Pastor, Basil, Jovian, Victorinus, Eugenia, Felicity, and Anastasia) (9 sets)
Group	XLI	St. John the Evangelist (2 sets)
Group	XLII	The Holy Innocents (2 sets)
Group	XLIII	Ember Masses (5 sets)

The system of enumeration of the formulae adopted through-out is that used by L. C. Mohlberg (*Sacramentarium Veronense*, Rerum Ecclesiasticarum Documenta, Series Major, Fontes I, Rome 1956).

As has been pointed out, the Sacramentary opens in the course of set vi of Group VIII, which is to be found in the month of April. The whole section consists of 43 sets of Mass prayers, some sets containing as many as seven prayers (vii) whilst others contain only two (xi). Though there are four definite names men-tioned in this section (Tiburtius, Laurence, Gregory, Chryso-gonus), the contents of the prayers indicate that they rightly belong to the commemoration of a group of martyrs and/or confessors. Whether this is a feast of a particular number of martyrs whose names are in the missing title or whether it is just a Common of martyrs is difficult to establish. The prayers allude to the striving and suffering here on earth of the martyrs whom they commemorate and their present enjoyment of the heavenly bliss. Although the Masses are all assigned by the compiler to the Paschal season there is no direct reference to the triumph and victory of Christ in his resurrection. The Mass xxvi with its rubric 'Pascali (E) F SP' contains a preface which clearly belongs to Eastertide, with its reference to the lamb which has been slain for us. The Mass with which the Sacramentary opens (vi) mentions the name 'Tiburtius' in one of its prefaces (2); it is possible that he is to be identified with an authentic Roman martyr of the same name. The name of Laurence, a name highly esteemed in the city of Rome, appears in Mass xx (72). It is difficult to see why, if this is the Roman martyr, the prayer (or the whole Mass) has not been placed in group XXI with the other Laurentian Masses; alternatively it may be another martyr with the name Laurence; though it may be an example of the formula's being accidentally misplaced. A name a little more difficult to identify is that of Gregory, mentioned in Mass xxxiii (126). It appears again later in the Sacramentary in conjunction with Chrysogonus (group XXXVIII). Whether the two references to the name Gregory both indicate that the same person is to be understood is again open to question, though Bourque argues that the two names taken in conjunction (i.e. Gregory and Chrysogonus) provide the clue to the origin of the two sets of prayers within which their names occur.[1] Finally there is the Mass 'IN DEDICATIONE' (xxxiv) 130–3 which contains in each of the four prayers a reference to the Apostle Peter. Feltoe argues that the Mass belongs to the dedication of the basilica to that apostle in Rome itself, whilst Bourque more convincingly suggests that the basilica in question is some way out of Rome.[2] The last Mass of this section concludes the month of April.

The seven sets for the feast of the Ascension, entitled PRAECES IN ASCENSA DNI, form the opening section of the month of May. Here, except in the first Mass (169–174), the number of formulae for each set is much smaller. In this group, however, the proper prefaces are more extended than those contained in the previous

---

[1] Bourque, op. cit., p. 112.   [2] Cf. pp. 87 ff.

sets of formulae. Clearly the theme is the exaltation to the heavenly kingdom of Christ the Saviour after his resurrection and the fervent hope of the faithful Christian that he might follow the same path after death.[1]

Five sets of formulae are assigned to the Vigil of Pentecost. The first two are entitled ORATIONES PRIDIE PENTECOSTEN and from their contents it is obvious that they are to be used on that day. The fifty days of Paschaltide are about to be completed as the Church awaits the outpouring of the gift of tongues (191). Since Pentecost was the other great festival (Easter Eve being the most important occasion) upon which baptisms were performed from the second century onwards, it is not surprising to find in this section the title IN PENTECOSTEN ASCENDENTIBUS A FONTE followed by prayers appropriate to the title. After a proper 'Communicantes' for the feast of Pentecost there comes a prayer of blessing over the milk and honey (205)—a feature of the baptismal rite known to Hippolytus also.[2] A similar prayer occurs in later manuscripts[3]. The title IN IEIUNIO QUARTI MENSIS seems rather out of place at this point and is more appropriately placed lower down, before the prayer 226. At the same time it has been pointed out that the prayer 'Concede nobis, domine . . .' (207) not only resembles the language used in Pope Leo's sermon for the Embertide at Pentecost but is actually used in other sacramentaries on these or other Ember-days.[4]

The feast of Pentecost has three sections, one of which is entitled CONTRA INIMICOS CATHOLICAE PROFESSIONIS. References in the prayers of this Mass, particularly the first (218), are considered to relate to the attack of the Vandals on Rome at Pentecost A.D. 455.[5] The other two Masses are concerned with the events of the first Pentecost—thanksgiving to God for the outpouring of his Holy Spirit upon the Church.

As was noted above, the ember season of Pentecost now follows. Considerable similarity exists in the first prayer (226) and

[1] Cf. pp. 99 ff.

[2] G. Dix, O.S.B., The Apostolic Tradition of Hippolytus (London), 1937, p. 40.

[3] This same prayer is found in the tenth-century Pontifical of Egbert of York (Paris, B.N. lat. 10575) and in the eleventh-century Pontifical from Setz (Paris, B.N. lat. 820).

[4] L. C. Mohlberg, Liber Sacramentorum Romanae Aeclesiae ordinis anni circuli (Sacramentarium Gelasianum), Cod. Vat. Reg. 316 / Paris Bibl. Nat. 7193, 41/56, Rerum Ecclesiasticarum Documenta, Series Maior, Fontes IV (Rome, 1960), formula 631.

[5] See below, p. 58.

the proper preface (229) with Leo's Sermons;[1] the same in fact as has been shown in connection with prayer 207. The Ember Mass brings to an end the month of May.

Group XIII begins the month of June with five Masses for the feast of St. John the Baptist. There is a similarity throughout the Masses in that the baptismal theme pervades them all, and especially Mass iv (247–50), which is preceded by the title, AD FONTEM. The special theme of this Mass and its prayers is the figure of the new birth and life conferred by baptism. It has been suggested that this Mass has a particular connection with the Lateran basilica[2] and the title marks a station which is made at the chapel of St. John Baptist in that basilica; this suggestion is made after a comparison of a similar Mass in the Gregorian Sacramentary.[3]

Eight sets of Mass prayers follow for the feast of the two brothers John and Paul, who were traditionally 'praepositus' and 'primicerius' respectively to Constantia, daughter of Constantine the Great. The whole of Mass i is repeated from Mass xxxix, ii from xl and iii from xli of the April collection. It is only in Mass v that both names John and Paul are mentioned.

A much larger number of Mass sets, 28 in all, are assigned to the feast day of SS. Peter and Paul. The Masses themselves present many interesting features for the study of the Sacramentary. There are a large number of phrases and in some cases prayers which occur as often as four times within this single section.[4] It seems clear that there has been some actual editing of the texts which appear in this particular section.[5] The names of the apostles Peter and Paul appear frequently in the prayers and their aid is implored in ruling and governing the Church. There is much in this section to suggest a Roman origin for the

---

[1] The formula 226 contains almost verbatim the language of Leo, Sermo lxxviii. 1 (Migne, *P.L.* 54. 416). The formula 229 similarly has close affinities with Leo, Sermo lxxviii. 3 (Migne, *P.L.* 54. 417).

[2] See below, pp. 88 ff.

[3] H. A. Wilson, *The Gregorian Sacramentary* (Henry Bradshaw Society, London, 1915), pp. 84–5. The Mass for the feast of St. John Baptist in this Sacramentary contains a prayer entitled 'Ad Fontes'. But see also below, p. 89 n. 3.

[4] Cf. the formula 310 'Vere dignum qui aeclesiam tuam in apostolica . . .' is paralleled in 296, 332, and 369.

[5] Cf. pp. 123 ff., where the editing of one particular set of parallel formulae is examined.

prayers—a certain authority in ecclesiastical affairs by the Roman Church is also indicated. After the first Mass there appears another title, CONIUNCTIO OBLATIONIS VIRGINUM SACRATARUM, followed by a prayer related to that title. A decretal of Pope Gelasius confines the consecration of virgins to the feast of the Epiphany, Easter Monday, and the feast of SS. Peter and Paul.[1] There is a similar rubric in the Gelasian Sacramentary.[2] The set xxi, which contains a section of prayers headed IN IEIUNIO, is the only one in the whole group of Masses which does not specifically mention the name either of Peter or of Paul, but speaks in terms of 'omnium apostolorum' and seems therefore to belong more properly to the feast of All the Apostles, which the Gelasian Sacramentary (Vat. Reg. 316) celebrates on the octave day of SS. Peter and Paul.[3] The proper preface (354) of this set is the only place in the Leonianum where the word 'trinitas' appears; it is also striking in the similarity of its imagery with a passage from St. Augustine.[4] It has been suggested that a number of allusions in the Masses (e.g. 282) indicate that the Church for which the particular prayers were composed is threatened by false teachers of some kind who are preaching false doctrines.

The month of July has only one feast-day; that with which the group opens, the feast of the seven sons of St. Felicitas, who are supposed to have been martyred in the reign of Antoninus Pius (c. A.D. 150). There are nine sets of formulae; in the third of these (385–9) there appears the title IN IEIUNIO, which seems only to apply to the succeeding prayer and proper preface (386–7); the other prayers are appropriate to a feast of martyrs, as are those which precede and those which follow them. This is followed by a long series of varied prayers entitled INC ORATIONE SET PRAECES DIURNAE which forms one of the most interesting sections in the book. There are forty-five sets of Mass prayers attached to this group. It would be fair to say that there are two categories into which most of the Masses could be placed, though

---

[1] Cf. P. Jaffé, *Regesta Pontificum Romanorum*, vol. i (1885), p. 636, col. 12.

[2] Mohlberg, *Sacramentarium Gelasianum*, p. 124, section CIII immediately before the proper 787. The rubric reads: 'Consecratio sacrae virginis, quae in Epiphania, vel secunda feria Paschae, aut in Apostolorum natalicio celebratur.'

[3] Mohlberg, *Sacramentarium Gelasianum*, p. 147.

[4] A similar line of thought is followed by Augustine: *Enarr. in Pss.* lxxxvii. 1 and IV (Migne, *P.L.* 37. 1103 f.).

by the very nature of the case these categories must remain rather fluid. On the one hand in the civil sphere many references in the prayers suggest a state of war and siege, of victory implored and victory gained; and on the other hand a state of turmoil within the Church itself is suggested. Numerous appeals to charity and patience are balanced by no less numerous and ardent denunciations of the unjust and scandalous adversaries. Because of the many and varied references pertaining to the historical situation of the time, this section has attracted a great diversity of interpretation in regard to date and circumstance, not only with reference to the barbarian attacks on Italy and more specifically upon Rome, but also with reference to the precise nature of the conflict within the Church. The question of the authorship of many of the prayers has also given rise to a number of theories; but, even if agreement cannot be reached as to the compiler of the different sets of Mass formulae, it can perhaps be allowed that the section is by no means a unity; a number of hands can be detected in its composition.[1]

The month of August opens with nine sets of Mass formulae, which are entitled N SCI STEFANI IN CYMETERIO CALLISTI VIA APPIA. This, in addition to the fact that it appears at the beginning of the month of August, would lead one to assume that the person being commemorated is Pope Stephen, the martyr (d. A.D. 257). In fact none of the Masses makes any reference to him at all; it is quite plain that the Masses properly belong, in the liturgical order of the year at least, to the day after Christmas Day, i.e. to the feast of St. Stephen, protomartyr, and it is to the protomartyr that the prayers refer. It may be that, as in other parts of the Leonianum, the prayers have fortuitously appeared under the wrong title. Another alternative explanation suggests itself—that some confusion has occurred at this point between the feast of St. Stephen, pope and martyr (2 August), and the feast of the Finding of St. Stephen, protomartyr (3 August), caused by the introduction of this latter fourth-century feast into the Western liturgy at some point.

The seven Mass formulae under the title NATALE SCI XYSTI IN CYMETERIO CALLISTI ET FELICISSIMI ET AGAPITI IN CYMETERIO PRAETEXTATE VIA APPIA and one complete Mass with the title IN NATALE SANCTORUM FELICISSIMI ET AGAPITI are undoubtedly

[1] See below, pp. 54 ff.

connected in some way with the burial-places of those whose names they bear. The first seven Masses appear to pertain to Xystus since his name alone is specifically mentioned, whilst the Mass with the title bearing the names Felicissimus and Agapetus mentions them by name in the preface (736) only.

Next come fourteen sets of Mass formulae for the feast of St. Laurence, one of the most famous of the martyrs of the city of Rome. There are frequent allusions in the prayers to the method of his execution and to the distribution which he made to the poor of the wealth of the Church. The Masses i, x, and xii seem to be more suitable for use on the Vigil of the feast, and the last Mass is prefaced by the words 'Item alia. ad octavas'. It is evident from the exalted tone of the prayers that the feast was celebrated with great solemnity.

The following section entitled IDUS AUG N SCORUM YPOLITI ET PONTIANI illustrates, to a lesser extent, a misplacing of prayers similar to that seen in the Masses of St. Stephen. Unlike the title, the first Mass mentions St. Hippolytus only (792), whilst the second mentions St. Agapetus by name in the fourth prayer of the Mass (798). The compiler, it would seem, being anxious not to change the text of any of the prayers, merely placed this title above the two Masses; no doubt he obtained this title from the calendar which he was using as a guide to setting out the various groups in some sort of order.[1]

The month of August ends with seven sets of prayers for the feast of SS. Adauctus and Felix. The first Mass is the only one proper to the day; it seems also wholly unique. Whereas the names appear in the title in the order Adauctus and Felix, in the prayer 181 they appear in the opposite order. The last preface (set vii, formula 823) looks as if it really belongs to the feast of an apostle; in fact there is a phrase of this prayer which occurs frequently in the prayers for the feast of SS. Peter and Paul.[2]

The section entitled XVIII KAL OCTOB N SCORUM CORNELI ET CYPRIANI contains two Masses of these saints who were commemorated together in the catacombs of St. Callistus and appear together on a mural in that same burial-place. Preceding the

---

[1] Feltoe suggests that the name 'Agapiti' of this collect be possibly interpreted as 'Hippolyti', op. cit., p. 100 n. 10.

[2] The phrase in question is 'orbis terrarum', which is a common combination of words in several of the prayers in the group for the feast of SS. Peter and Paul; cf. pp. 126 ff.

proper preface of the former Mass (826), the title appears PCES
H IN SCAE EUFYMIAE, which, it has been suggested, indicates a
'station'; but clearly the most reasonable suggestion is that the
preface is misplaced and this is an indication that its proper
position is with the formulae following.

Three sets of formulae are assigned to the feast-day of St.
Euphemia. In addition there is also the proper preface (826),
which has been placed too early in the course of a Mass of SS.
Cornelius and Cyprian. Much of the fame of St. Euphemia in
the West was due to the fact that the Council of Chalcedon
(A.D. 451) was held in a church which bore her name. It is unknown at what date a church was dedicated to her in Rome, but
there was certainly such a church in existence near St. Puden-
tiana, since mention is made of its being repaired by Pope Sergius (A.D. 687–701). The three sets of formulae can hardly have
been composed much before the beginning of the sixth century,
since it is possible to recognize the influence of the 'Passion of
St. Euphemia'. This lengthy account, of little value historically,
is of a late date and recounts the series of tortures inflicted upon
the martyr, and the intervention of the Devil. It is chiefly the
victory of this feeble woman over the infernal serpent which is
joyfully proclaimed by the proper prefaces of the first two sets
of Mass prayers.

The anniversary of a basilica, dedicated to the honour of St.
Michael the Archangel, is the occasion of the five sets of prayers
which follow the title PRID KAL OCT N BASILICAE ANGELI IN
SALARIA. None of the sets of prayers forms a complete Mass, but
this is not a new feature in the Leonianum; four of the five
sections mention the name of Michael with praise and honour
(846, 847, 854, 858); the third Mass seems more general in its
application, i.e. perhaps a feast of the Angels—it does not
specifically mention St. Michael. It is likely that the prayers are
in some way connected with the basilica of St. Michael on the
Via Salaria in Rome; however, they would not appear to belong
to the feast of his appearing on Mt. Garganus, since there is no
reference to this in the prayers of the section.

There follows a rather complex section of Mass prayers with
the general title ADMONITIO IEIUNII MENSIS SEPTIMI ET ORATIONES
ET P. It is worthy of note that the majority of the fourteen Masses
in this section are like many in the Gelasian books, having three

prayers—two collects and a secret—before the preface. Again in these Masses, which are penitential in their content, some have seen references to attacks upon Rome. It has also been suggested that the Mass 867–71, because of its contents, really belongs to a time nearer the Christmas festival. Perhaps it belongs more properly to the subsequent section—INVITATIO PLEBIS IN IEIUNIO MENSIS DECIMI—for which there are six sets of Mass prayers, again of a penitential nature. One prayer in Mass xi (923) is of particular interest; it seems appropriate to the harvest season, as does the preface in Mass xii (929). Immediately following the opening title there is a single collect followed by eight sets of prayers. Mass vi has the words 'In ieiunio' inserted after the opening collect, so too does Mass vii, whilst Mass viii has the same words written before the opening prayer.

After the penitential section there follows group XXVIII: CONSECRATIO EPISCOPORUM, BENEDICTIO SUPER DIACONOS, CON-SECRATIO PRESBYTERI. It is maintained by Dom B. Botte[1] that the pure Roman rite of ordination is preserved in the texts which are to be found in the Sacramentary. There are no indications of actual rites in the Leonianum but only forms of prayer. One single idea is retained in the preface for an episcopal consecration—the bishop is the high priest of the New Testament. The prayer for the ordination of priests is divided into three parts. 1. God himself organizes the hierarchy of sacred functions. 2. This is applied to the Old Testament (Moses and the seventy elders, Aaron and his two sons), then to the New Testament (disciples are associated with apostles). 3. The invocation is made to God by the bishop, who has need of helpers also. The role of the priest is clearly defined:

ut cum pontifices summos regendis populis praefecisses, ad eorum societatis et operis adiuventum sequentis ordinis viros et secundae dignitatis eligeris.   (954.)

The formula for the diaconate begins by expressing the same principle as in the formula for the priesthood (1). After recalling the Levites of the ancient law, the prayer asks God to send the Holy Spirit so that the deacons might exercise their ministry in the sevenfold gifts of his grace.

A longer section (XXVIIII) entitled IN NATALE EPISCOPORUM

[1] *The Sacrament of Holy Orders* (Eng. edn., London, 1962), p. 8.

follows containing twenty-three Masses, of which eight only really pertain to the anniversary of an actual episcopal consecration. Of these eight, Mass v is a collection of prayers only and no proper preface appears at all. It has been suggested that these are the anniversary Masses of Pope Vigilius, but other alternative theories have also been put forward.[1] With Mass ix we seem to leave almost entirely the idea of episcopal anniversaries and to return to more general occasions.

The content of the remainder of the sets of formulae becomes more general. Like the contents of the group XVIII INC ORATIONES ET PRAECES DIURNAE they have been the subject of study in regard to their author. For the most part Gelasius and Vigilius emerge as the two to whom we must attribute the prayers.[2] Chavasse considers that many of the sets are to be placed in the year A.D. 538 after the deliverance of Rome from the siege in that year.

Groups XXX and XXXI are entitled AD VIRGINES SACRAS and INC VELATIO NUPTIALIS respectively. The first is to be used at the consecration of virgins: the prayer gives praise to God, the author and giver of chastity, and goes on to mention the fall of man and his restoration through the Word who was born of the Blessed Virgin, herself obedient to the call of God. The prayer ends with a list of the duties which the newly-consecrated virgin is called upon to perform. The second of the groups, the Nuptial Mass, opens with two prayers, followed by a proper 'hanc igitur' (presumably this would be used in the appropriate place during the Canon); two further prayers lead into the actual prayer of blessing. God the creator, who, as in the story related in Gen. 2:21–4, made a friend in the form of woman for Adam by taking his bone in order to create Eve, is now implored to bless this woman who is about to take her marriage vows— fidelity to this vow is enjoined and the prayer continues that those qualities found in Rachel, Rebecca, and Sara might also be found in the bride now being blessed.

The opening of the month of October (section XXXII) is chosen by the compiler of the Sacramentary as the appropriate place for the prayers entitled DE SICCITATE TEMPORIS, but only the immediately succeeding prayer seems to come directly under this head; and there appears to be no reason why the month of

[1] See below, pp. 78 ff.   [2] See below, pp. 116 ff.

October should be connected with drought. Both the marginal note and the first prayer of Mass iii seem to suggest the end of the Lenten season. On the other hand the prayer 1135 of Mass vi ('Deus qui remedia salutis . . .') perhaps suggests a feast of the apostles, whilst the succeeding preface belongs either to Easter or to a Requiem and in view of the next section it is likely that the latter is correct.

Five Requiem Masses follow: the first is a common Mass for the departed—clergy or laity; the second is for a person dying in a state of repentance. The first three prayers of Mass iii appear to be variants of or supplements to Mass ii, whilst the last four prayers of this same Mass perform a similar function for Mass i. The fourth Mass is for a deceased bishop as also is the fifth. Since the name of Laurence appears in Masses iv and v it has been suggested by the Ballerini that they commemorate some bishop of Rome who died within the octave of St. Laurence; it is certainly worthy of note that in three of the prayers the name of Laurence (as well as 'episcopi' for 'sacerdotis') should at this point be substituted for the 'illius' of the same prayer in the Gelasian Sacramentary.[1] Since Xystus III (A.D. 432–40) is said to have been buried near St. Laurence[2] and the Ballerini calculate that his death occurred on 18 August A.D. 440, it is inferred that Xystus III is meant. Section XXXIII entitled SCI SILVESTRI, which is a Mass for Pope Silvester, is suggested by the Ballerini to be the Mass of his Deposition and placed by the compiler at the end of the Masses SUPER DEFUNCTOS.

Section XXXV contains two Masses, as the title indicates, for the festival of the 'Four Crowned Ones', though it is by no means certain which particular saints are intended, since there were two groups, one of four and another of five, which the Roman Martyrology for 8 November gives. The prayers themselves do not give any indication since no proper names are mentioned; they could be applied to any group of Christian martyrs.

[1] Mohlberg, *Sacramentarium Gelasianum*, formulae 1643, 1655, 1644.

[2] The *Liber Pontificalis* (i. 235) states of Xystus III: '. . . qui etiam sepultus est Via Tiburtina in crypta iuxta corpus beati Laurenti.' An inscription, visible in the ninth century, near the choir of the basilica of St. Laurence, mentioned the repair and rebuilding of the church by the priest Leopardus, in the time of Pope Zosimus. De Rossi believes that the three niches in the vestibule of this reconstructed basilica were occupied by Zosimus (*Lib. Pont.* i. 225), Xystus III (*Lib. Pont.* i. 235), and Hilary (*Lib. Pont.* i. 245).

St. Cecilia, one of the greatly venerated martyrs of the early Roman church, is assigned five sets of Mass prayers. Reference is made in the proper preface of Mass i (1172) to Valerian whom she married; it was he as well as his brother that she converted. She herself suffered martyrdom after them. The prayers themselves are very rich in their praise of her and her acts—they obviously originate in a church where her esteem was high. Whilst the prayers do give a considerable amount of information regarding the life of St. Cecilia, at the same time they do contain much of what is 'apocryphal'; making no mention of the actual conversion and martyrdom of her husband Valerian.

Section XXXVII with its title VIIII KAL DEC N SCORUM CLEMENTIS ET FELICITATIS is followed by four Masses which only mention Clement. These four sets of prayers tell how he sets himself a voluntary exile and goes on his self-imposed journeyings: far from his homeland he finds his parents again and converts them, and he is finally called to occupy the chair of Peter in Rome. The allusions to St. Clement of Rome's life in all these prayers seem to be consistent with the account given of him in the Clementine Recognitions. The last three Masses of the whole section are preceded by the title IN NATALE SCAE FELICITATIS to whom reference has already been made in respect of her sons in the title at the opening of the month of July. Whilst the first two sets of formulae make direct mention of Felicitas, the last (iii) is the only one of the section which is adapted to the two saints conjointly, as the heading indicates, and even here the preface applies only to St. Felicitas: none of the forms in this set seems to appear elsewhere.

It is difficult to identify the Gregory mentioned in the title of the following Mass, and actual knowledge of Chrysogonus, whose name is in the Canon of the Mass, is very sparse. As we remarked earlier, the name Gregory may possibly designate the person who also appears in one of the April Masses.

The 30 November is given over to the feast of St. Andrew, with four sets of prayers, the third of which appears to be a Vigil. The feast is of the apostle who is Peter's brother by his birth, by his faith, by his apostolic office, and by the glory of an identical death on the cross (1226). Allusion is also made to the well-known scene, popularized by his Passion, of the apostle's sermon to the people on the occasion of his martyrdom (1230, 1236).

The month of December naturally contains the Christmas Masses and it is with these that the month opens. There are nine Masses for the feast of which i and v belong more properly to the Vigil of Christmas than to the day itself. The formulae appear under a rather complex title: VIII KAL IAN N DNI ET MARTYRUM PASTORIS BASILEI ET IOUANI ET VICTORINI ET EUGENIAE ET FELICITATIS ET ANASTASIAE. There is much of interest within this section, especially the profusion of Biblical quotations which occur in the proper prefaces of sets ii and iii (1245, 1247). The prayers sound a note of joy and triumph that the Incarnate Word of God has come to tread underfoot the devil and his works and to redeem mankind from the power of evil. The first formula of the whole section (239), 'Deus qui humanae substantiae . . .', has found a permanent place in the Offertory prayers of the Mass at the commixture of water and wine in the chalice.[1] The phraseology in the first prayer of Mass vi (1258) and the preface (1260), also the preface of Mass vii, are all reminiscent of Leo's style. The latter preface especially seems directed against Eutychianism.

Two sets of formulae for the feast of St. John the Evangelist follow, presumably celebrated on 27 December. The second preface, like the first, is extended somewhat, and quotes the Prologue of the Fourth Gospel in what seems to be an attempt to teach the truth about the relation of the Word to the Father. It might be possible that some form of Monarchianism or Subordinationism was being attacked. On the following day the Holy Innocents are given two sets of Mass prayers, when again both the prefaces give details of the slaughter of the children, the preface of the second Mass (1291) recalling the Matthean account of the event as it quotes Jer. 31: 15 in this context.

The Sacramentary closes with section XLIII entitled IN IEIUNIO MENSIS DECIMI, which corresponds to the Advent Embertide and should therefore properly precede sections XL–XLII. This is a further example of the confused manner in which the material has been brought together in the manuscript. As was pointed out in the description of the manuscript above, the very last part of the Sacramentary 1330–1 is a later, seventh-century, addition to the actual text of the Leonianum.

[1] See below, p. 98.

4

THE CALENDAR

THE titles of the various groups of sets of Mass formulae require a separate section for consideration. These form the liturgical calendar of the Leonianum. Unlike any present-day prayer book where the temporale appears first and the sanctorale follows, the Leonianum contains a scheme of arrangement in which the temporale and the sanctorale are mixed together throughout the course of the year. The headings themselves have in all probability been taken from an independent calendar and then used in accordance with the collection of formulae which the compiler had in hand. Some of the headings in the Leonianum, unlike those to be found in the Gelasian and Gregorian Sacramentaries, give very full information regarding the place of burial of the saints and martyrs they commemorate.

As we have already noted in the description of the Sacramentary, one method of arrangement of the material is by groups of sets of formulae, each assigned a number and a title. It is with these titles that this section is concerned; they form the Calendar of the Leonianum. The title for the group of Masses with which the Sacramentary opens is missing; thus the first title in the book appears at the opening of the month of May—PRAE-CES IN ASCENSA DNI—the remainder of the month is occupied with this feast, the Vigil of Pentecost, and the feast of Pentecost.

The title N SCI IOHANNIS BAPTISTAE indicates not, as is usual in such titles, the heavenly birthday of the harbinger of the Lord, but his earthly birthday. It was one of the feasts which found its place in the earliest of the Church's calendars on this day (24 June). It is found in the Hieronymian martyrology where the point about the earthly birthday is particularly stressed. The Carthaginian calendar reflects the same usage, and one of the greatest writers of North Africa, St. Augustine, attests the same in two of his Sermons.[1] Duchesne considers that the feast had its origins in the West.[2] In the Roman Calendar, as he points out, there is an exact parallel between this feast and the feast of the Nativity of the Lord—'octavas kalendas Julii': 'octavas kalendas Januarii'. It is likely that the place of origin of the formulae in the Leonianum is Rome and that they can be dated about the beginning of the sixth century. The reasons for this are given in another section.[3]

St. John and St. Paul together (26 June) are the patron saints of the 'titulus Pammachii' or 'Byzantis' on the Coelian Hill. This building of Pammachius must be given a date in the early years of the fifth century, before his death in A.D. 410. The 'acta' of these saints are wholly unreliable. It is possible that the title 'Byzantis' indicates an earlier foundation on the same site, since the remains of a house of about the third century have been found underneath a church. The dedication of the church to these saints is not attested until the early sixth century, evidence for which can be found on a tombstone (A.D. 535). Frere[4] considers the mention of their names in the Roman Martyrology a dubious one; in fact it is probably not a genuine entry of Roman martyrs, but one borrowed from liturgical or ecclesiastical sources. The sets of formulae in this group contain one only which mentions them by name (v). The first formula (269) informs us that the two saints were brothers in faith and in martyrdom, and the proper preface (271) indicates that their relics could be found in the city itself. All we can be sure of is that the early incorporation of their feast into the calendar is clear and that the names of the two saints were of considerable import in Rome.

The saints of the Roman Church *par excellence* are Peter and Paul. But this feast day (29 June), shared by them both, does not rely upon a history of their deaths, since they were possibly martyred in two different places outside Rome, and possibly at different times also.[5] The Liberian Catalogue mentions for this day—'Petri in catacumbas et Pauli Ostense, Tusco et

---

[1] Augustine, *Sermones*, cclxxxvii, cclxxxviii (Maurist edn., Paris, 1838), vol. 5. ii, cols. 1692 and 1694.   [2] Duchesne, op. cit., p. 271.   [3] See below, pp. 88 f.

[4] W. H. Frere, *Studies in Early Roman Liturgy*, vol. 1 (The Kalendar) (Alcuin Club Collections, Oxford, 1930), p. 108.

[5] O. Cullmann, *Peter—Disciple, Apostle, Martyr*, English edn. by F. V. Filson (London, 1953), pp. 151–2. Cf. also Batiffol, *Cathedra Petri* (Paris, 1938), p. 174.

Basso consulibus' (A.D. 258). These apostles are the only martyrs of the Roman Church who are listed in the third-century Catalogue. Frere suggests that the addition of the consular date is unusual and that it probably records the institution of the joint festival. The Hieronymian martyrology, however, states: 'Romae, Via Aurelia, natale sancti Petri et Pauli apostolorum, Petri in Vaticano, Pauli vero in via Ostensi, Utrumque in Catacumbas, passi sub Nerone, Basso et Tusco consulibus.' Delehaye[1] and others consider that the remains of the two apostles were buried on the Vatican Hill and that there they have remained undisturbed. Others, however, suggest that a temporary burial-place was found on the Appian Way until preparations for a more fitting permanent resting-place could be completed on the sites of their respective martyrdoms. Recent excavations beneath the basilica of St. Peter's, Rome, tend to indicate that it is almost impossible to identify the actual burial-place of Peter; no excavation work has yet been done under the church of St. Paul on the Via Ostiensis, and so no conclusion can yet be reached about the burial-place of Paul.[2] Throughout the formulae of the whole group found in the Leonianum the two names are always found together. Though undoubtedly their place of origin is Rome, the date of these formulae depends upon other historical data mentioned within them which is dealt with in another section.[3]

July the tenth is the day upon which the Seven Brothers were commemorated. July has this one feast only assigned to it. The seven sons of St. Felicitas are supposed to have been martyred in the reign of Antoninus Pius (c. A.D. 150). There is, however, no record of a persecution during this reign; but it is related that public calamities such as a famine, an inundation of the Tiber, earthquakes in Asia Minor, ravaging fires at Rome, Antioch, and Carthage stirred up the mob to seek the favour of the pagan gods by the shedding of Christian blood.[4] It is prob-

---

[1] H. Delehaye, Les Origines du culte des martyrs, 1933, pp. 264 ff.

[2] On this problem see H. Chadwick, 'St. Peter and St. Paul in Rome: The problem of the Memoria Apostolorum Ad Catacumbas', J.T.S. 8 (1957), esp. p. 32, where he points out that the crux of the problem is still the relation of the double shrine on the Via Appia to the two individual memorials, the one to St. Peter on the Vatican, the other to St. Paul on the Via Ostiensis.

[3] See below, pp. 57-8.

[4] W. M. Ramsay, The Church in the Roman Empire (London, 1893), pp. 331-4.

able that in some such way Felicitas and her children suffered without any participation on the emperor's part. From about the middle of the fourth century seven martyrs were commemorated on 10 July as our title reveals: NATALE SCORUM MARTYRUM FELICIS PHILIPPI IN CYMETERIO PRISCILLAE VITALIS ET MARTIALIS ET ALEXANDRI IN CYMETERIO IORNARUM ET SILANI IN CYMETERIO MAXIMI VIA SALARIA ET IANUARII IN CYMETERIO PRAETEXTATE VIA APPIA. This indicates that Felix and Philip were buried in the cemetery of St. Priscilla, Martial, Vitalis, and Alexander in the cemetery 'Iornarum', Januarius in the cemetery of Praetextatus, and Silanus (Silvanus) in the catacomb of Maximus. It was in 1863 that de Rossi discovered, in the cemetery of Praetextatus, a frescoed chapel with a 'graffito' invoking St. Januarius. It is suggested that the close proximity of the tomb of St. Silanus in the catacomb of Maximus to that of St. Felicitas[1] may have given rise to the identification of the seven martyrs as her sons and therefore as brothers. The title of this sacramentary commemorates the seven as martyrs, making no mention of Felicitas or of the fact that they were brothers. One of the formulae of that group (398), however, does name them as brothers, but this is no doubt influenced by the account given in the 'acta'— the only source in which this information is to be found—which are certainly to be dated no later than the sixth century. Since the title makes no allusion to the fact that they were brothers, it is likely that it comes from an earlier tradition which represents the seven merely as martyrs, without any ties of kinship. The problem is further confused by an obvious parallel with the Seven Maccabees. The formula of the Leonianum referred to above (398) is found in the Gregorian Sacramentary as a collect for the Seven Maccabees.[2] The early cultus connected with these saints is attested by the Liberian Catalogue, an epitaph of St. Damasus, and the Hieronymian martyrology, all of which associate them as brothers. Except for one reference in the Leonianum, mentioned above, there would have been no reason to suppose that either the prayers or the title had their origin on the commemoration

---

[1] Both Silanus and Felicity were buried in the same cemetery; the catacomb of Maximus was also known as 'ad Felicitatem'.

[2] *The Gregorian Sacramentary*, ed. Wilson, p. 282. (Found in Codex Ottobonianus 313.)

day of seven martyred brothers. The only thing which can be said positively is that the day is one which commemorates the seven men who are named and the only thing which they had in common was that they were martyred on the same day. Thus it is suggested that the title represents an earlier and distinct tradition of the local Roman congregation, probably about the early fourth century.

August the second is the occasion of N SCI STEFANI IN CYME-TERIO CALLISTI VIA APPIA. The day should rightly belong to the feast of Pope Stephen, who died in A.D. 257. His name occurs in the Liberian Catalogue in the 'depositio episcoporum' and not among the martyrs. However, all nine sets of Mass formulae belong to St. Stephen, protomartyr. Obviously the compiler has misplaced the sets of formulae, but this confusion could be the clue to the manner in which the difficulty may be resolved. The last of the nine sets mentions a basilica dedicated to the honour of the protomartyr:

> Vere dignum: hac festivitate laetantes, quo dicata nomini tuo basilica beatus Stefanus martyr suo honore . . . (701.)

In fact, of the basilicas erected by Pope Leo I and Pope Simplicius[1] and dedicated to St. Stephen none has any relation to Pope Stephen; both are dedicated to the protomartyr. The former basilica was built by the virgin Demetrias during the pontificate of Leo (A.D. 440–61) on the Via Latina.[2] The remains of this basilica were unearthed in 1858. However, it is in the same basilica that the feast of Pope Stephen was observed, as is shown by the note 'via Latina' added on this day in some sacramentaries. The Liber Pontificalis also gives the information that Pope Simplicius (A.D. 468–83) dedicated a church to St. Stephen, protomartyr, on Mons Caelius, but the more celebrated basilica was that built in the time of Pope Leo I and it is more probable that this is the one referred to in our formula. It is certain that Pope Stephen was buried in the catacombs of Callistus. In the middle of the fifth century his tomb was quite accessible there. Sixtus III (A.D. 432–40), we are told by the

---

[1] Duchesne, Lib. Pont. i. 238 and 249.

[2] 'Leo natione Tuscus . . . sedit annos 21 . . . Huius temporibus fecit Demetria ancilla Dei basilicam sancto Stephano via Latina miliario iii, in praedio suo' (Lib. Pont. i. 238).

Liber Pontificalis,[1] 'constituit . . . et platoma in cymeterio Calisti ubi commemorans nomina episcoporum'. It is this list of martyrs and bishops buried in the catacombs of Callistus, reconstructed by de Rossi, which mentions Pope Stephen. The 'Gesta Stephani', written during the sixth century, locate the burial place of Pope Stephen 'ad cymeterium sanctae Lucinae . . . qui appelatur hodie cimiterium Callisti', whilst his so-called companions are buried on the Via Latina. Stephen was honoured for a long time as a bishop of Rome; no mention was made of his being a martyr. The Gospel-list of Würzburg states: 'Die ii mens aug. nt. sci. Stephani pontificis'.[2] The *Liber Pontificalis* records a basilica dedicated to him on the Via Latina which commemorates only the fact that he was pontiff and does not mention anything about his being a martyr; this point is made in the biography of Pope Leo IV.[3] By the mid eighth century the local feast of Pope Stephen had not attained so great a degree of importance and popularity for it to have found a place in the so-called Gelasian Sacramentary, preserved in the manuscript Vat. Reg. 316.[4] Some would date the extension of his cult and its introduction into the liturgical life of the Roman Church about the middle of the sixth century. It is difficult to establish the exact date in view of the late development of the 'Gesta Stephani'. It is easy to explain the mention of the burial-place of Callistus in the title to this section, and from the contents of the formulae it is likely that the introduction of the cult of Pope Stephen to the basilica of Demetria is indicated; hence the end of the fifth century is a possible date, and this conclusion is more likely in view of the feast's omission in the Gelasian Sacramentary—it is a purely local observance. On the other hand, if the compiler's interest is not purely local, but is rather concerned with those saints especially honoured by the Roman Church, whose cults are already widespread in the city and its surrounding area, then clearly the formulae in this group must be assigned to a later date (the middle of the sixth century).

[1] Duchesne, *Lib. Pont.* i. 234.

[2] Cf. G. Morin, 'Liturgie et basiliques de Rome au milieu du viii siècle d'après les listes d'évangiles de Wurzbourg', *Revue bénédictine*, 28 (1911), p. 311.

[3] Duchesne, *Lib. Pont.* ii. 116, '. . . basilica beati Stephani Pontificis via Latina, milliario tertio . . .'

[4] It is, however, found in two other important 'Gelasian' manuscripts, Rheinau 30 and St. Gall 348.

A second title for a group of Mass prayers, similar in nature to one which has already been discussed, appears in August: NATALE SCI XYSTI IN CYMETERIO CALLISTI ET FELICISSIMI ET AGAPITI IN CYMETERIO PRAETEXTATE VIA APPIA. In this group there are seven sets of formulae taken from different sources; the compiler does not appear to distinguish clearly between the 'comites Xysti', buried in the catacombs of Callistus (i.e. the four deacons mentioned by St. Cyprian[1] and named by the *Liber Pontificalis*), and Felicissimus and Agapetus. There seems to be a rather confused tradition about the number of persons present at the death of Xystus and the number of those who died with him. The tradition that his two deacons Agapetus and Felicissimus were buried in the cemetery of Callistus is supported by an inscription round the tomb 'mi refrigeri Januarius, Agapetus, Felicissimus'. This inscription was written round the tomb about a hundred years later, during the pontificate of Damasus. The Roman martyrology (6 August) mentions four sub-deacons Januarius, Magnus, Innocent, and Stephanus as also having been beheaded and buried in the cemetery of Praetextatus with Felicissimus and Agapetus, whilst it rightly describes that of Callistus as the resting-place of the bishop himself. All the evidence which points to the fact that Xystus suffered martyrdom on 6 August and was buried in the catacomb of Callistus is remarkably early and conclusive. The title of this group in the Leonianum agrees with early tradition in placing Felicissimus and Agapetus in the cemetery of Praetextatus, whilst the *Liber Pontificalis* is no doubt mistaken in adding the four Roman sub-deacons to the names of Felicissimus and Agapetus. St. Xystus himself was one of the most highly venerated among the popes martyred after St. Peter; his name also occurs in the Canon of the Mass. Undoubtedly the place of origin of these formulae is the city of Rome. Whilst Xystus is the only name mentioned in the Gelasian Vat. Reg. 316, the Leonianum, following the Liberian Catalogue, indicates that the seven sets of formulae for St. Xystus are followed by one for SS. Felicissimus and Agapetus. Frere argues[2] that the association of the two is more likely to be the result of topographical

---

[1] St. Cyprian, *Ep.* lxxx. 1. 4: '. . . Xistum autem in cimiterio animadversum sciatis viii id. Aug. die et cum eo diacones quattuor.'

[2] Frere, op. cit., p. 122.

and liturgical features, since the cemetery of Callistus where Xystus lay is not far from that of Praetextatus, the resting-place of the others; both are on the Via Appia. It is here suggested that the fact that all were martyred on the same day has been the dominating influence, as well as the similarity of the circumstances of the martyrdom of all of them.

St. Laurence has been, since the fourth century, one of the most highly venerated of Roman martyrs in the Roman Church: his name occurs in the Canon of the Mass and in the Litanies. It is known that he was buried in the cemetery of Cyriaca 'in agro Verano' on the Via Tiburtina.[1] In the reign of Constantine a chapel was built over his tomb and the *Liber Pontificalis*[2] records that this was enlarged by Pope Pelagius II (A.D. 579–90) into a basilica—the present San Lorenzo fuori le Mura. In the Leonianum fourteen sets are provided of which xii is more suited to the Vigil and xiv to the octave day of the feast. It is worthy of note that the Gregorian Sacramentary provides two sets for this day;[3] but no doubt the explanation of this fact is to be found in the existence of two adjacent churches dedicated to St. Laurence which were not finally combined until the pontificate of Honorius III in the thirteenth century. It is difficult to suggest an exact date for the formulae; it may be that in view of the construction of a chapel in the mid fourth century at the burial-place of Laurence a number of liturgical forms would have resulted; this would certainly provide a *terminus a quo*.

The two names mentioned by the title N SCORUM YPOLITI ET PONTIANI are both saints of the Roman Church, Pontianus being Pope from A.D. 230 to 235, and Hippolytus, having rejected Pope Callistus as a heretic, seems to have set himself up as an anti-pope. Both were deported in the persecution of the Emperor Maximin (A.D. 235–8) and were exiled together in Sardinia, where they died after forced labour in the mines. Their remains were brought back to Rome on the same day, Pontianus being buried in the catacombs of Callistus and Hippolytus in a tomb on the Tiburtine Way. The Liberian Catalogue states:

Pontianus ann. V m lld vii fuit temporibus Alexandri a cons. Pompeiani et Pelagiani. Eo tempore, Pontianus episcopus et Yppolitus

[1] Duchesne, *Lib. Pont.* i. 181.
[2] Ibid. 309.
[3] *The Gregorian Sacramentary*, ed. Wilson, pp. 94–5.

presbyter esoles sunt deportati in Sardinia in insula nocina [*sic*]
Severo et Quinto cons. . . .

In the Depositio Martyrum we find 'idibus Augusti Hippolyti
in Tiburtina et Pontiani in Callisti'. However, the prayers which
are to be found here do not correspond very well with the title.
The first set mentions St. Hippolytus only, whilst the second
mentions St. Agapetus by name in the fourth formula (798).
A name which springs to mind at once is Agapetus, the Pope
from A.D. 535 to 536, a staunch defender of the faith. There
seems to be the same sort of confusion here as is found in connection with the feast of St. Stephen; the compiler, who is anxious
not to change the text of any of the prayers, merely places the
title above the two sets of formulae. The formulae and the calendar are, in all probability, entirely independent. This peculiarity
may, however, enable us to date these Masses with some degree
of accuracy. Of the cemetery of Hippolytus, near the basilica of
St. Laurence, to which set i directs, there only exists the basilica
of St. Agapetus, erected by Pope Felix III (A.D. 483–92).[1] It is
suggested that this factor has led to the combination of the two
sets of formulae. But the Agapetus mentioned here cannot be
Pope Agapetus, since this is before his pontificate and death;
furthermore, his feast day is kept on 22 April. The Agapetus
commemorated here is more likely to be the saint whose place
of origin is Praeneste (Palestrina), about thirty miles east of
Rome.[2] There is a similar close connection of the city of Rome
with its immediate surroundings in the case of St. Euphemia,
to whose honour Pope Gelasius dedicated a basilica at Tibur,
north-west of Praeneste. The cultus of St. Agapetus is attested
not only by mention in the sacramentaries in this month, but
also by traces of the ruins of the basilica dedicated to him in
Praeneste and an epitaph which bears his name. In the eighth
and ninth centuries several other churches took his name for their
title. The appearance of the name Agapetus in the formula 798
has been said to be a slip for Ypoliti or Pontiani, which seems
a very unlikely explanation; it may be, however, that the compiler has not adapted the prayer to the particular saint, as has
occurred in other parts of the Sacramentary. It is of interest to

---

[1] '. . . iuxta basilicam sancti Laurenti martyris' (Duchesne, *Lib. Pont.* i. 252).
[2] Feast-day, 18 August.

note that the Gelasian Sacramentary (Vat. Reg. 316) uses this same prayer for the feast-day of St. Hippolytus on 23 August, substituting 'Ypoliti' for 'Agapiti'.[1]

The feast of SS. Adauctus and Felix (30 August) presents yet another celebration of the local Roman community which has become part of the universal calendar of the Western Church. In the Leonianum, out of the seven sets of formulae provided, only the first is proper to them. The Hieronymian martyrology lists them under the title 'Romae natale sancti felicis adaucti'. However, as 'Felix and Adauctus, in the cemetery of Commodilla on the Ostian Way' are mentioned in the Depositio Martyrum of A.D. 354, this is reliable evidence for the existence, at an early date, of their cultus. Without doubt the place of origin of the formulae within this group is Rome and a *terminus a quo* of the early fifth century is suggested.

Both the title and the two sets of formulae of group XXIV associate together the names of Pope Cornelius and St. Cyprian. Pope Cornelius had been buried and received great honour in the crypt of Lucina, very near the catacombs of Callistus along the Via Appia. Earlier sources of information indicate that originally the two saints' days were celebrated separately. The Depositio Martyrum (*c.* A.D. 354) mentions Cyprian only: 'Cypriani, Africae, Romae celebratur in Callisti.' On the other hand the Roman calendar, at the beginning of the fifth century, only knows of Pope Cornelius' being remembered at Rome on that day, as can be inferred from the text of the Hieronymian martyrology: 'Romae natale Corneli et depositio dionisi episcopi et in kartagine cypriani espiscopi . . .' Cornelius was not in fact buried in the catacomb of Callistus, where Cyprian was honoured, but his remains were placed in a different area, quite distinct, known as the crypt of Lucina, but near the catacomb of Callistus.[2] Pope Cornelius, however, died in June. Either the 14 September is the date of his translation or we may have to look elsewhere for the explanation; it may, indeed, be purely fortuitous. In the pontificate of Leo I there is still evidence that the two saints were possibly even then honoured separately.

[1] L. C. Mohlberg, *Sacramentarium Gelasianum*, formula 985: 'Sancti Ypoliti martyris, Domine quaesumus . . .'

[2] 'Cuius (Cornelii) corpus noctu collegit beata Lucina cum clericis et sepelivit in crypta, iuxta coemeterium Callisti, via Appia, in praedio suo, xviii Kal. Octob.' (Duchesne, *Lib. Pont.* i. 151).

Pope Leo I built a basilica above the crypt of Lucina, near the catacomb of Callistus, but dedicated it to St. Cornelius only.[1] No trace of this basilica now remains. It is mentioned in two itineraries of the seventh century but not later.[2] Frere suggests that the joining of the two commemorations must be attributed to Pope Leo, who had built the basilica at the burial place of Cornelius.[3] The Liberian Catalogue directed the commemoration of St. Cyprian to take place in that same cemetery. Thus Frere concludes: 'Cornelius provided the place and Cyprian the date.'[4] Both the Gelasian and the Gregorian Sacramentaries commemorate the two together. The present Sacramentary exhibits the same characteristics, which at least provides a *terminus ad quem* as far as the date is concerned. In view of what has been said it is possible to suggest that the formulae themselves can hardly have been written much before the end of the fifth century.

Following the group of Mass formulae for the feast of SS. Cornelius and Cyprian there are three sets for the feast of St. Euphemia (16 September); there is also a preface which has been misplaced and is to be found amongst the previous formulae. This is indicated, however, by the insertion PCES H IN SCAE EUFYMIAE immediately before the formula (826). This date, of course, is that observed by Rome and subsequently by the Western Church as a whole. The Eastern Church keeps the feast on 13 April, as does the Gelasian Vat. Reg. 316.[5] Apart from the fact of her martyrdom there is nothing whatsoever known about the saint; her 'acta' are wholly unreliable. Her cultus was widespread from an early date. No doubt the fame attributed to St. Euphemia in the West was due in some measure to the fact that the Chalcedonian Council of A.D. 451 took place in a church dedicated to her. It is recorded in the *Liber Pontificalis* that Pope Gelasius dedicated a church to St. Euphemia 'in civitate Tiburtina'.[6] The basilica at Tivoli (Tibur), just east of Rome,

[1] 'Fecit autem basilicam beato Cornelio episcopo et martyri, iuxta cymiterium Callisti, via Appia' (Duchesne, *Lib. Pont.* i. 239).

[2] Ibid. i. 241 n. 9.

[3] Frere, op. cit., p. 129.

[4] Cf. Bourque, op. cit., p. 126, where he suggests that the author of formula 832 seems to go out of his way to justify the mention of the name Cyprian alongside that of Cornelius: '. . . tuamque in sanctis martyribus Cornelio simul etiam Cypriano praedicare virtutem . . .'

[5] Mohlberg, *Sacramentarium Gelasianum*, section xv, p. 136.

[6] Duchesne, *Lib. Pont.* i. 255.

disappeared at an early date. There was, however, a church in Rome itself with this dedication (on the Vicus Patricius near St. Prudentiana), which after the sixth century was used as a monastery. The building is first attested in the *Liber Pontificalis*,[1] in which it is stated that Pope Sergius (A.D. 687–701) had the roof repaired after it had been for some time with no roof at all. The occurrence of the feast at this point in the Leonianum is of considerable importance. It is known that only in Rome and its environs was the feast kept on this day. Outside Rome the feast was usually observed on 13 April. It can therefore be concluded that the place of origin of the formulae certainly follows the Roman tradition and the date that can be assigned to them is the second half of the fifth century.

Michaelmas, as the title in the Leonianum indicates—N BASILICAE ANGELI IN SALARIA—is the occasion of the dedication of a basilica on the Via Salaria. This is the basilica of the Via Salaria which is mentioned in the 'Epitome libri de locis sanctorum martyrum' by de Rossi (Via Salaria Nova):

per eandem quoque viam venitur ad ecclesiam S. Michaelis septimo milliario ab urbe.

Similarly, there is a note in the Hieronymian martyrology to this effect:

Romae, via Salaria, milliario VII, dedicatio sancti Michaelis.

Having originated in Phrygia, where the archangel was chiefly venerated as a healer, the cult of St. Michael the Archangel soon spread to the West and found its way into the liturgy at a comparatively early stage, as can be seen from the five sets of formulae which follow this title in the Leonianum. The cult in the Western Church received a strong impetus from the famous apparition on Mount Garganus in the pontificate of Gelasius (A.D. 492–6), in commemoration of which a feast day is still observed in the Roman Catholic Church on 8 May. The September feast is retained in the Gelasian and Gregorian Sacramentaries. De Rossi is of the opinion that this basilica had been constructed towards the middle of the fifth century; before this date, he maintains, there can be no question of its existence; also the dedication inscriptions of the martyrology are all of this

[1] Duchesne, *Lib. Pont.* i. 375 and 380 (note 9, on text of p. 375).

period.[1] He points out that the extract from the Hieronymian martyrology is not the archetype but an Italian insertion into the original text. The mention at this point of the apparition on Mount Garganus is a very late interpolation. The last addition made to the text of the Hieronymian martyrology in Italy is to be dated *c.* A.D. 470. The end of the fifth century can be suggested as a possible date for the composition of the formulae in this section and their origin assigned to the basilica of St. Michael on the Via Salaria seven miles out of the city. Two churches of later date lying within the city presumably superseded the suburban church when it disappeared; the one enlarged by Pope Symmachus (A.D. 498–514)[2] and the chapel in the burial-place of Pope Hadrian, established in the seventh century.

One of the martyrs greatly revered in the early Roman Church is St. Cecilia, whom we find commemorated on 22 November in the Leonianum. Some of the formulae indicate, by their contents, that the information contained in her 'acta' was known by the compiler. The 'acta' are altogether untrustworthy and are to be assigned to the latter half of the fifth century. Hence the formulae must be later than this date, and are probably to be assigned to the early part of the sixth century.[3] The remains of Cecilia had previously been buried in the catacombs of Praetextatus before being moved by Pope Paschal I (A.D. 817–24) to the church in Rome which bears her name. There is, however, a considerable amount of debate as to who exactly St. Cecilia was. No mention is made of a Roman virgin martyr named Cecilia in the period immediately following the persecutions, nor does her name occur in the fourth-century 'depositio martyrum'. It may be that originally her cultus was centred round the burial-place of Cecilia, the foundress of the church, the 'titulus Caeciliae' which in later times became known as the 'titulus Sanctae Caeciliae'.

The title which follows, N SCORUM CLEMENTIS ET FELICITATIS, combines the two names of Pope Clement and St. Felicity for

---

[1] J. B. de Rossi, *Bullettino di Archeologia*, 2 Serie 2 (1871), p. 146.

[2] Duchesne, *Lib. Pont.* i. 262.

[3] Cf. J. A. Jungmann, S.J., *The Mass of the Roman Rite*, vol. 2 (American edn., New York, 1955), pp. 118–19. Here he points out that the more developed prefaces contain almost a précis of the saint's life and work such as can be found in formulae 1172, 1178, 1180, and 1183.

commemoration on 23 November. Four sets of formulae are given to St. Clement and two to St. Felicity; whilst the last combines the two. In all the last three sets reference is made to the sons of St. Felicity (see above). There is no early tradition or record of the date of Clement's death. The Liberian Catalogue does not mention him. It may well be that his name had become associated with the 'titulus Clementis' (c. A.D. 390) as a patron—Frere suggests the day may be the festival of that church, but there is no evidence to support this statement.[1] St. Felicity mentioned here, following Kennedy,[2] is to be identified with the Felicity of the Canon of the Mass. Undoubtedly she is a Roman martyr and this is attested by the 'depositio martyrum' of the Liberian Catalogue for 10 July. According to her 'acta' she was martyred with her seven sons. Pope Boniface I (A.D. 418–22) built an oratory over her tomb.[3] De Rossi has identified the cemetery of Felicity with a catacomb and a group of tombs to the right of the Via Salaria about a mile from the city. The oratory of Boniface is mentioned in itineraries of the seventh century, although no traces of it are now to be found. It is likely that the formulae concerned with St. Clement originated in the church in Rome bearing his name, and that similarly with St. Felicity the place of origin was the catacomb of Felicitas on the Via Salaria.

Though the heading N SCORUM CHRYSOGONI ET GREGORI indicates that the day is to celebrate two saints, the set of formulae, has no reference to any named martyrs or saints. The name 'Gregori' at this point has been connected with the same name in the April group, but this is unlikely. No satisfactory explanation of the name has yet emerged. Frère makes the point that quite certainly this feast has its origin in an urban church and not in a suburban 'martyrium'.[4] There is a martyr of this name who belongs to Aquileia who was greatly venerated in Northern Italy. Whether he can be identified with the Chrysogonus mentioned in our title is open to question. Certainly this is an observance of the local Roman community;[5] the

---

[1] Frere, op. cit., p. 141.

[2] V. L. Kennedy 'The Saints of the Canon of the Mass', *Studi de antichità cristiana,* xiv (1938), pp. 164–8.

[3] Duchesne, *Lib. Pont.* i. 227.   [4] Frere, op. cit., p. 142.

[5] Chrysogonus must have been of importance to the Roman community since his name appears in the list of saints at the opening of the Canon of the Mass.

titular church of Chrysogonus in Trastevere is mentioned in
A.D. 499. It is also called 'titulus sancti Chrysogoni' in an inscription of A.D. 521. Like Cecilia, the name of the person connected with the construction of the church may have been the
first association and only later did this name become involved
with the martyr of Aquileia. Though it can be said that the formulae have certainly come from Rome, it is difficult to suggest
any definite date.

Four sets of Mass formulae are provided in the Leonianum
for the feast of St. Andrew, one of which is suitable for use on
the Vigil. During the pontificate of Simplicius (A.D. 468–83) the
church called 'Catabarbara'[1] was founded; this served as the
ancient church of St. Andrew in Rome.

The title which appears for 25 December reads VIII KAL IAN
N DNI ET MARTYRUM PASTORIS BASILEI ET IOUIANI ET VICTORINI ET
EUGENIAE ET FELICITATIS ET ANASTASIAE. The Nativity of the
Lord is mentioned and it is with this that the following nine
sets of formulae are concerned. The seven martyrs, Pastor,
Basilius, Jovian, Victorinus, Eugenia, Felicitas, and Anastasia,
receive no further mention. Little is known about the four men
except that Basilius and Jovian were said to have been buried
on the Via Latina. Eugenia was a Roman martyr, buried in the
catacomb of Apronianus on the Via Latina. Felicitas is said
to have been martyred in Milan. Anastasia was martyred at
Sirmium in Pannonia and from there her relics were translated
to Constantinople in the mid fifth century. Thus it was that her
cultus spread and in Rome became attached to the 'titulus Anastasiae' (again possibly named after its foundress), the church
near the Circus Maximus which had its origin during the pontificate of Damasus (A.D. 366–84). Hence the dedication was
taken to mean the martyr of Sirmium. It was in this church
that the Papal stational Mass of the Dawn on Christmas Day
was celebrated; a commemoration of St. Anastasia is still made
at this same Mass in the Roman Rite.

From the evidence which has been presented in the discussion
above it may be suggested that the compiler of the Leonianum
has extracted the headings of the groups of Mass prayers from

[1] Duchesne, *Lib. Pont.* i. 249 and 250 n. 2. This church was originally a secular
hall, erected by the consul Junius Bassus during the reign of Constantine. This is
the first mention of a public building's having been appropriated by the Church.

an existing Calendar which reflects the use of the local Roman community. Especially is this seen in the more extended titles which indicate the catacombs in which the earlier martyrs were interred. The more extended headings are not found in later sacramentaries. The arrangement of the various groups is clearly governed by the volume of material which the compiler has available. There are only two major feasts of the Lord— His Nativity and Ascension—which find a place in the calendar. This feature, however, is not surprising, since the first part of the manuscript is lost. There is also the feast of Pentecost which has a Vigil, and the feast of the Holy Innocents. The number of Apostles is small; four only are mentioned, Peter, Paul, Andrew, John the Evangelist, together with John the Baptist. Thus eighteen other items of the calendar make up the rest of the Sanctorale and these are purely local observances from the city of Rome. The date of the actual material placed within any particular group depends upon a number of factors; but where possible a date has been suggested. The calendar itself clearly reflects an earlier stage of development than does the material which is arranged within it.

5

HISTORICAL REFERENCES IN THE LEONINE SACRAMENTARY

PERHAPS one of the most striking features of the Leonine Sacramentary, and one which will receive further comment later, is the large number of sets of formulae which are often assigned to a particular feast. The very fact of the existence of so large a number of sets for any one occasion indicates a situation in which the liturgy and liturgical prayer generally must have been very much more fluid than at the present time. Consequently it would appear that a great deal of the liturgical prayer of the Church was much more pertinent to the particular occasion in the life of the community within which and for which that prayer was offered. It is not surprising therefore that when the city of Rome was besieged such a period of turmoil and distress should be reflected in the prayers of those Christians living in and around that city. A number of prayers which could only have been written within the context of hostile invasion have found their way into the Leonianum; our task is to examine them more closely and attempt to discover the possible date and occasion of such compositions.

There are a large number of formulae in the Sacramentary which make quite explicit allusion to the times in which the Roman people were besieged, surrounded by their enemies, and exposed to massacre and pillage. Others express thanksgiving to God after victory or deliverance. The group which probably contains the largest number of formulae in which such references are made is that entitled XVIII ORATIONES ET PRAECES DIURNAE. It is this group also which contains the largest number of sets of formulae within the whole Sacramentary—forty-five in all. In addition to a large number of references alluding to some internal disruption within the Church itself[1] there is this second theme which reflects a state of war. We must now go on to

[1] See below, pp. 66 ff.

examine in more detail some of the allusions. The actual sets within which there are references to the topic of war are as follows: vi, vii, ix–xiii, xxv–xxxii, xxxiv–xliv.

It is among a number of general statements on the perils of war that some more precise indications occur from time to time. Within the formulae 443–8 (set vi) particular reference is made to the hostilities of the invaders:

> Vere dignum: agnoscimus enim . . . ad peccantium merita perti-
> nere, ut servorum tuorum labore quaesita sub conspectu nostro mani-
> bus diripiantur alienis, et quae desudantibus famulis nasci tribuis,
> ab hostibus patiaris absumi . . .   (446.)

Duchesne[1] has argued that this preface reflects the anxiety felt by the people during the siege of Rome A.D. 537–8. Vitiges had mustered some 150,000 men to besiege Belisarius in Rome. For a whole year he made exhaustive attempts to capture the great city. In the year A.D. 537 the Ostrogoths, encamped outside the city, reaped the harvest which had been so carefully prepared by the Roman people. Now the Romans could only look on, helpless, as the invaders ravaged the countryside. It is unlikely that the prayer quoted above is alluding to the sieges of Rome either by Alaric or by Genseric,[2] since these took place too late in the year when the harvest would be over. Again, in these two sieges it was the city itself which was the main centre of attack rather than the surrounding countryside. However, as Duchesne rightly points out, a fact which should be kept in mind through-out this inquiry is that the Romans were often besieged during the wars with the Goths and later during the Lombardic invasions. Because the indications in the Sacramentary are often far from explicit or precise, it is impossible to say quite definitely that it was this particular siege (A.D. 537–8) by Vitiges which is actu-ally reflected in our formulae (443–8). On the other hand it may be said that the reference here (446) is not wholly inconsistent with the account of the circumstances of that siege which we have from independent sources.[3]

---

[1] L. Duchesne, *Christian Worship* (Engl. translation, 5th edn., London, 1931), pp. 137–8.

[2] Alaric besieged Rome in August A.D. 410 and Genseric in May/June A.D. 455.

[3] The very reliable independent witness of contemporary events is to be found in the writings of Procopius of Caesarea. See below, p. 61 n. 1.

It is possible, however, to be more positive in the conclusions which can be drawn from the formulae of set xxviii, especially from formulae 570:

> Munera nomini tuo, domine, cum gratiarum actione deferimus, qui nos ab infestis hostibus liberatos paschale sacramentum secura (placida) tribuisti mente suscipere: per.

One very noticeable feature is that this set of formulae has no connection with the month of July, but ought to be placed in the Paschal season. This is a further example of the misplacing by the compiler of a formula which is repeated in numerous other places in the Sacramentary. Since the sieges of Rome by Alaric, Genseric, and Ricimer were all conducted in the summer months it is impossible to look to these as likely events to which the set of formulae (569–73) can be attributed. As was said previously, Vitiges spent a whole year in his efforts to take the city of Rome. During this time, another Roman army, which had landed on the Adriatic coast early in A.D. 538, was occupying Picenum. The Archbishop of Milan requested the Greek troops to make an invasion of Liguria, which they did, seizing the great North Italian town. When this news was brought to Rome, Vitiges, in despair, decided to abandon any further thought of attack on the city and withdrew. The danger which had been so imminent was now over and the Christian congregation was able to celebrate the Paschal solemnities in peace. Vitiges had retired from Rome in March A.D. 538 and the feast of Easter in that year fell on 4 April. The first formula of the set indicates the occasion at once:

> Magnificentiam tuam, domine, praedicamus suppliciter implorantes, ut qui nos inminentibus periculis exuisti . . .   (569.)

Chavasse,[1] in an attempt to give a more precise date to some of the sets of this group, has suggested Low Sunday A.D. 538, i.e. 11 April, as the occasion of this set. Those who favour any explanation other than a siege of Rome would have difficulty in interpreting formula 571 (the proper preface). Bourque,[2] however, does suggest a further possibility for the interpretation

---

[1] A. Chavasse, 'Messes du Pape Vigile dans le léonien', *Ephem. Lit.* 64 (1950), pp. 161–213.

[2] Bourque, op. cit., p. 87 n. (5).

of the phrase 'captivitatem quam extrinsecus summovisti'; it may well have been provoked by the advance of Alaric's troops as far as Aquileia in A.D. 401 and their overthrow at Pollentia in A.D. 402. But this explanation seems very unlikely in view of the place of this particular formula within the whole set, which clearly derives from the eagerly awaited deliverance just before Easter A.D. 538.

A more direct reference to Rome and the Romans is made in the formula 604. This formula is the first in what appears to be a sub-division of the large group. It is entitled INC PRAECES DIURNAE CUM SENSIBUS NECCESSARIIS. The formula begins:

> Omnipotens sempiterne deus, Romanis auxiliare principibus, ut tua virtute roboratis omnis hostilitas nec viribus possit praevalere nec fraude: per.

The formula 605 mentions the 'Romana securitas', whilst the preface of this set has the marginal note (probably added at a later date) 'de contumelia hostili, quae ad correctionem fidelium constat', and goes on to mention the resistance of the enemy and the help of God in vindicating those who remain faithful to Him. It is perhaps worthy of mention that the last formula of the set (609) has found a place in the Gelasian Sacramentary as a post-communion prayer entitled 'in tempore belli'.[1] But there are also other formulae similar to that first mentioned (604) within the Leonianum itself; and in addition to these two formulae in which the word 'Romanus' appears, there are a further nine in which the same word appears, though in different forms. One particularly is indicative of the sudden attack of Genseric in A.D. 455 upon Rome; the proper preface (361) of set xxiii of group XV is very similar in its content to a sermon preached by Pope Leo[2] on the octave day of the festival of the apostles Peter and Paul, in which he comments upon the small number of people present at the feast of these saints. The proper preface brings before us a picture of a city which has already been humiliated many times under the attacks of its enemies. Though it would seem from the tone of the sermon that it was preached some time after the event, it nevertheless reflects, as

[1] Mohlberg, *Sacramentarium Gelasianum*, formula 1502.
[2] Leo, *Sermo* lxxxiv, 'In octavis apostolorum Petri et Pauli; de neglecta solemnitate' (Migne, *P.L.* 54. 433).

does the preface, the ungratefulness of the Roman people in their neglecting this festival, even though it was the anniversary of their deliverance from the terror and distress caused by the sudden attack of the Vandals upon the city in A.D. 455. Dom G. Morin, however, attempts to show that Leo's sermon was preached on the anniversary of the capture of Rome by Alaric;[1] but it would seem likely that this commemoration had already fallen into disuse by the time of Pope Leo.

The other references, being much less definite in their indications of a particular historical context, are consequently more difficult to assign to a precise date. However, in spite of the fact that references such as these are more general and vague, a number of attempts, not altogether convincing, have been made to give them a definite date. Feltoe[2] considered that the formulae mentioned above (604, 605) have parallels in 218, 553, and 480, in that similar phrases occur in each of them:

... sic hostes Romani nominis et inimicos catholicae professionis ... (218.)

... Romani nominis ubique rectores ... (553.)

... et religionis integritas, et Romani nominis securitas ... (480.)

The first phrase is taken from formula 218, which is to be found in the group of Masses pertaining to Pentecost. Nevertheless this set has its own sub-title CONTRA INIMICOS CATHOLICAE PROFESSIONIS. Undoubtedly such a title is of little help in placing this set of prayers within its historical context. As has been mentioned above, Rome was taken by a sudden attack in A.D. 455, and it is in this year that the feast of Pentecost occurred on 13 June—the Vandal leader having entered the city on 2 June and pillaged it for fourteen days until 16 June, which occurred during the octave of the feast of Pentecost.

Though the second and third phrases quoted above, taken from the formulae 553 and 480, are themselves similar, yet it cannot be agreed that they originated in the same siege of Rome. The formula 553 appears in set xxv, in which the third formula

---

[1] Alaric had besieged Rome in A.D. 408, 409, and 410. On 24 August 410 Rome was conquered for the first time by a Gothic king.

[2] Feltoe, op. cit., p. 195 (note on p. 77, l. 6 'Romanis principibus—Romana securitas').

(555) is one particularly suited to the Paschal season. It is useful to note that in the Missale Romanum this same prayer is to be found as the post-communion for the Thursday in Easter Week.[1] It is suggested, then, that the set (553–7) has come from a time when Rome was in a state of siege during the Paschal season. The 'rectores Romani nominis' everywhere are prayed for in formula 553; prayer is offered also that the 'pax populi' might be secured. Whilst it is suggested here that formulae 553–7 pertain to the siege by Vitiges, others have seen in this set a situation parallel to that found in formulae 479–85 and 218–21. Hence, the siege by Alaric (A.D. 410) has been suggested as the occasion of all three sets of formulae. Certainly the parallel in formulae 480 and 218 is close, but 553 seems to have some other situation in mind. A further problem is created, when a close analysis is made, by the omission of a proper preface in set xxv so that following the prayer 555 there are simply the letters P F E SP, which are undoubtedly some rubrical direction, the meaning of which still remains obscure, though as we shall see several suggestions have been made.[2] It is clear that the two formulae 218 and 480 mention parallel subjects, 'religionis integritas' (480), 'catholicae professionis' (218), 'Romani nominis securitas' (480), and 'hostes Romani nominis' (218), whilst 553 mentions nothing of 'religio' but prays for 'rectores Romani nominis' and 'pax populi'.

Thus, following this discussion of the three sets of formulae (553–7, 479–85, 218–21), it is suggested that the set of formulae 553–7 should be assigned to the year A.D. 537, whilst the remaining two sets (479–85, 218–21) be placed in the context of the attack of Genseric upon Rome in A.D. 455. However, it would be well to keep in mind the words of Duchesne which were mentioned at the opening of this chapter. So far, the sieges of Rome both by Genseric and by Vitiges have been suggested as having provided the occasion of our formulae. The formulae themselves have not supplied clear evidence which would enable them to be unquestionably assigned to either of the sieges. At the same time, it may be said that such evidence as is provided is not out of keeping with the accounts of these sieges which have come from other reliable and independent sources.

---

[1] Cf. also *The Gregorian Sacramentary*, ed. Wilson, p. 63.

[2] See below, Appendix A, pp. 145–53.

Thanks for continued guidance and protection are offered in set xiii of this group. The set could almost be called a Mass of Thanksgiving:

Quaesumus, omnipotens deus, ne ad dissimulationem tui cultus prospera nobis collata succedant, sed ad gratiarum actionem tibi propinsius exhibendam potius nos semper accedant: per.   (487.)

The other formulae all speak of thanksgiving and deliverance; the proper preface (489) is particularly joyous in its note of thanks to God. The post-communion formula (490) suggests some great festival: 'Observationis annuae celebritate gratulantes ut eorum, quorum actionibus inheremus, plenis effectibus gaudeamus: per.'[1] (490). The last formula in the set could possibly be taken to give a hint of the Paschal season. In the Gelasian Vat. Reg. 316[2] it appears as the formula 'ad populum' for the first Sunday after Pentecost, whilst in the Ambrosian Missal the occasion is Wednesday in Easter Week. Clearly the set is a thanksgiving after some period of stress; it is therefore suggested that this set is to be dated shortly after the departure of Vitiges from Rome; the formulae 569–73, as it has already been pointed out, almost certainly indicate the Paschal time of the year, in which Vitiges departed from Rome. The sentiments expressed in the formulae of the present set (xiii) indicate that this too belongs to the same season. It is very difficult to imagine that the annual feast envisaged by formula 490 is any other than the great solemnity of Easter; and in the case of this set (xiii) the suggested year is A.D. 538.

In the May of A.D. 536 the Strait of Messina was crossed by Belisarius, whilst one of Justinian's generals conquered Dalmatia. He was enthusiastically welcomed by the Italian people as a liberator; in turn he seized Naples and occupied Rome unopposed on 10 December A.D. 536. The Ostrogoths, however, still possessed more determination and energy than the Vandals. When reports reached them of the first defeats, even before the fall of Rome, they deposed their ruling chief, Theodahad, and elected Vitiges, the bravest of their warriors, into his place. It was with great skill that Vitiges united all his forces

[1] This prayer itself seems defective as it stands; Feltoe suggests it is meant for a form of 'communicantes'. Feltoe, op. cit., p. 63 n. 4.

[2] Mohlberg, *Sacramentarium Gelasianum*, formula 682.

and set off for his attack against the city of Rome. The actual events of the siege are not fully known. It began properly on 23 February A.D. 537; seven encampments were established round the city and all the aqueducts leading to the city were taken. The effects of such measures upon the Roman people are obvious. The people themselves were not thoroughly accustomed to the evils of war nor to the conditions such as those in which they now found themselves. Procopius[1] relates that the Roman people took for granted the sudden fall of the city, at the same time looking helplessly on as the Ostrogoths laid waste their fields. In July of the same year both soldiers and citizens were affected by the famine and plague which ravaged the city. Reduced to their last extremity many of the people urged Belisarius to fight; but help sent by the Emperor was already on its way and between August and October troops landed and assembled at Naples to march northwards to Rome. There then followed a short period of calm in which a treaty was negotiated between both sides and hostages were exchanged. Skirmishes and clashes continued and it was plain that the siege could not be long delayed. On 4 March A.D. 538 the siege was raised and a great massacre at the Milvian Bridge ensued.[2] This was one year and nine days after the arrival of the Ostrogoths before the walls of Rome.

This brief account of the siege of Rome by Vitiges provides some indication of the state of mind of the Roman populace and the calamities which those same people endured. The main themes of the formula 553, mentioned above, appear once more at a later stage in the same group. The two themes 'rectores Romani nominis' and 'pax populi' are paralleled in the formula 590, where prayer is made on behalf of 'statum Romani nominis' and 'pax salusque perpetua tuorum populorum'. A similar situation is envisaged by the formula 660 in its appeal for the defence of the 'rectores Romani nominis'. The account of the city in a state of siege with the people themselves divided in their loyalties

---

[1] Procopius, *De Bell. Goth.* i. 1–24, ii. 2–10.

[2] Disillusioned by the seemingly insurmountable difficulties in assaulting the walls of Rome, Vitiges decided to abandon all hope of attack and ordered a retreat to be made. His armies departed along the Flaminian Way. Seeing this, the Roman leader, Belisarius, ordered the Gothic armies to be pursued. The Milvian Bridge was the scene of the encounter of the Roman armies with the rear of the retreating Gothic forces.

and the leader of the Roman armies himself opposing some of the policies put forward by Constantine provides a convincing account against which these formulae may be viewed. However, the meticulous system of dating the various sets of formulae which is made by Chavasse[1] is not altogether convincing. The group entitled DE SICCITATE TEMPORIS (XXXII) he ascribes to the beginning of the year A.D. 538. It is true that there was an exceptional drought at that time and there was a scarcity of water, made more acute for the Roman people by the seizure of their supplies from outside the city by the invaders. The formula 1111, the only one in the set which pertains to the title, could be assigned to that period. Sets ii–vi he places in Holy Week of the same year. This could be said of ii and with more certainty of iii with its rubric PROPE PASCA and the formula 1123 which obviously indicate the imminence of the Paschal feast. The formula 1128 of set iv mentions the 'Romani nominis' and prays for the people in a similar way to the formula 590. However, the proper preface (1130) reads as if it belongs to the feast of the Ascension or the Sunday following—where in fact it is placed in the Gelasian Sacramentary.[2] A further parallel to the formula 590 is to be found in 1132 of set v. The proper preface (1134) in this same set, with the appearance of such words as 'verbum', 'conditor', and 'reformator', seems to indicate the Christmas theme far more strongly than the Paschal. A comparison with formulae 1239 and 2358 confirms this view. Again, it is difficult to place set vi in Holy Week A.D. 537. It is true that the proper preface (1137) could relate to Easter; on the other hand it is also appropriate for use in the group following (requiem) as Feltoe points out.[3] The formula 1135 belongs to a Common of Apostles, and there is no definite indication in the second (1136) of the three formulae belonging to this set that it should also be placed in Holy Week. As has been demonstrated, the formulae 1128 and 1132 seem to reflect a historical context which is the same in both cases; also, it is further suggested that they are parallel to 590, which has already been ascribed to the year A.D. 537. It is possible therefore to conclude that A.D. 537 is the

---

[1] A. Chavasse (article referred to on p. 56 n. 1).

[2] Mohlberg, *Sacramentarium Gelasianum*, formula 589. Though the two prefaces are not exactly similar, it appears likely that they both have had the same origin.

[3] Feltoe, op. cit. 213 (note on p. 144, l. 27 'Deus qui . . .').

year to which these formulae also belong, but for the reasons stated above it is not easy merely to place them in Holy Week of that year. In all probability they have come from very different periods in the Church's liturgical year. One factor, however, which does appear to be constant in each of these sets is that the background of the formulae, so far as can be discerned, is not incompatible with the account given us by Procopius of the state of mind of the Roman people during the year of the siege, A.D. 537.

In this same article Chavasse proposes a connection between the fifteen sets of Mass formulae in group XXIX relating to the anniversary Masses of the consecration of Pope Vigilius and the forty-five Mass formulae which are to be found within the group which is at the moment under discussion, i.e. XVIII. If sixteen sets are eliminated, which Chavasse accepts for reasons of style and historical allusions are to be attributed to the hand of Pope Gelasius, there remain forty-four sets. These he considers were composed for use between 12/19 July A.D. 537 and 27 June A.D. 538. His conclusions, Chavasse states, are entirely confirmed by the allusions to the events of the siege of A.D. 537/8. The nine sets of group XXIX (x, xi, xii, xiv, xvi, xvii, xviii, xxi, xxiii) he assigns to certain Sundays following Easter Sunday (4 April A.D. 538) as far as 27 June. All the nine sets follow the deliverance of Rome from invading armies. Again, with reference to group XVIII, he suggests that the title INC PRAECES DIURNAE CUM SENSIBUS NECESSARIIS indicates the fact that the eleven sets following form a distinct division from the others of that group. With less convincing arguments than those he uses to put forward the ideas expressed above he suggests that this smaller group provides the Sunday Masses from 17 January to 28 March for the year A.D. 538.[1]

Another part of the Sacramentary brings before us certain formulae which undoubtedly have their origin in troubled times. The formula 716 appears in set iv of group XX in the month of August. The occasion is the feast-day of St. Xystus and his companions. Formula 716 reads:

Adesto, domine, supplicationibus nostris, et intercedentibus sanctis tuis ab hostium nos defende propitiatus incursu: per.

[1] Much of this information is set out by Chavasse in his article mentioned above, p. 56 n. 1.

The formula 719 contains a similar petition:

> Prodest quidem, domine, continuata censura peccantibus . . .

Again in set v the Lord is asked to grant that the feast-day of these martyrs might be celebrated in all safety:

> Praetende, domine, misericordiam tuam, et esto populi tui defensor et custus; ut sanctorum tuorum veneranda sollemnia securo possint frequentare conventu: per. (725.)

There is a third set (vii) in which the formulae mention and give thanks for the liberty which has been enjoyed throughout the years of danger. The Christian community has always been able to meet and celebrate the festival of St. Xystus:

> Deus, qui nos . . . ut sicut securis eadem mentibus, ita dignis celebremus officiis: per. (730.)

> Vere dignum . . . et martyris tui Xysti semper honoranda sollemnia nec inter praeteritas mundi tribulationes omittere voluisti, et nunc reddita prestas libertate venerari: per. (732.)

The set of formulae with the title IN NATALE SANCTORUM FELICISSIMI ET AGAPITI reflects the same sentiments:

> Vere dignum: qui . . . festa semper optanda fecisti celebrare gaudentes; et qui dedisti fidem inter adversa constantem, reddes beneficia (munera) libertatis: per. (736.)

The troubled conditions envisaged by the various formulae quoted above can most reasonably be assigned to the year A.D. 472, as Bourque suggests.[1] It was in the year A.D. 471 that civil war was imminent. Ricimer saw this as his opportunity and gathered his forces at Milan, whilst Anthemius was stationed at Rome. Yet again the same struggle for power between the Roman and barbarian parties was to be rehearsed. For a time the intervention of Epiphanius, bishop of Pavia, gave way to a temporary peace (that is, if the account of his biographer Ennodius is to be relied upon); but it was inevitable that such a struggle should lead to war. Thus in A.D. 472 war broke out. Early in the year Ricimer had marched on Rome and besieged the city with a large army. The siege went on for five months (February–July) and during this time the city suffered from

---

[1] Bourque, op. cit., p. 123.

famine. An army which had marched from Gaul, with the intention of relieving Anthemius, was defeated by Ricimer. This, coupled with an act of treachery, finally led to the fall of the city. It is suggested that the ferment and civil strife in the years A.D. 470 to 471 were the conditions which led the Christian community in Rome to compose such formulae as these for use in their churches. Regarding the Masses for the feast of St. Xystus and their historical references, it is known that Genseric had left Rome by 16 June after his sudden attack in A.D. 455 and Alaric had ravaged the city during the period 14–17 August (in A.D. 410). On this feast thanks are given for the deliverance vouchsafed to the people—the date is only 6 August. It is unlikely then that either the attack by Alaric is indicated, since the feast precedes the actual attack, or that of Genseric, which was preceded and followed by periods of relative calm. There would have been no barbarian encampments round the walls of Rome and access to the catacombs would not have been difficult.

The final fall of the Western Empire came in A.D. 476, Rome having been sacked, by Alaric and Genseric, on two previous occasions. The invading armies were Arian and could well have provoked violent opposition to the Roman See; however, even though they were Arian, their policy was one of toleration. A much greater disaster befell the city during the Gothic War (A.D. 537–53) when at one stage it was almost completely abandoned by its inhabitants. Thus, for much of the fifth century and a large part of the sixth, Italy was beset with foreign invaders. With the whole country in such turmoil it is hardly surprising to find reflections of the contemporary political situation in the prayers of the Christian community, especially when the prayers of that community were far more adaptable to the immediate situation than are our present forms. Bearing in mind the difficulties of ascribing particular formulae to particular dates, it has been suggested that the sieges of Alaric, Genseric, Ricimer, and Vitiges have been reflected in our formulae, with a particularly large number arising from the last which was really the opening of the Gothic War and a long struggle for the Roman Church until the pontificate of Gregory the Great (c. A.D. 540–604) when the papacy itself began to take over much of the political administration.

6

ECCLESIASTICAL CONFLICT

THE section XIV entitled INC ORATIONES ET PRAECES
DIURNAE, whilst it is one of the longest in the whole Sacramentary, is at the same time one of the most interesting. It is
perhaps because it contains so many formulae which are similar
in content and yet without precise reference to particular events
that it has provided such a rich field for so many to investigate.
Already much has been said concerning the Mass formulae
which relate in some way or another to a situation in which war
and strife predominate in the civil sphere. Interspersed among
these sets of Mass prayers are others which make clear reference
to dissension and strife within the Church itself; though again
the precise occasion is difficult to identify. The sets which contain clear references of such a nature are as follows: i–v, viii,
xiv–xxiv, xxxiii, xlv. At the same time it must be recognized
that sets xxxii, xxxiii, and xlv are difficult to assign with any
certainty to either of the two general themes of civil or ecclesiastical strife.

Before considering in more detail the formulae which contain
references to dissension within the Church we must make a
passing comment about set iv. The secret prayer (433) mentions
the dedication of the fruits of the earth, which God has commanded to be consecrated to Himself:

> Consecra, quaesumus, domine, quae de terrenis fructibus nomini
> tuo dicanda mandasti: ut et gratam tibi nostram facias servitutem,
> et sacramentum nobis perpetuae salvationis instituas: per.

The last part of the prayer mentions the 'sacramentum' of our
eternal salvation, which Bourque takes as an allusion to the
approaching feast of Christmas.[1] This he suggests because this
particular formula is similar in content to the proper preface
(923) in a set which appears in section XXVII in the month of

---

[1] Bourque, op. cit., p. 91.

September. This set of Mass prayers, though it is to be found in the month of September, does provide an effective link with December as the formula in question (923) illustrates. Indeed it appears in the group with the more general heading 'INVITATIO PLEBIS IN IEIUNIO MENSIS DECIMI', indicating a period of prayer and fasting for the December Ember season. The Sermons of Pope Leo[1] for the Ember Days of December contain passages which are probably not unrelated to our formulae, especially in respect of the thanksgiving for the fruits of the earth:

> Sancti patres nostri . . . decimi mensis sanxere ieiunium et omnium fructuum collectione conclusa . . . abstinentia dicaretur.   (xvi.)

> Decimi mensis solemne ieiunium . . . annua est consuetudine celebrandum quia plenum iustitiae est . . . gratias . . . agere . . . pro fructibus quos . . . terra produxit.   (xvii.)

In view of the close connection between the September set, illustrated by the proper preface (923) and the Sermons of Leo for the December Ember season, it is not surprising that the similarity in content of the formula (433) of set iv of the group XVIII and the proper preface 923 has led Bourque to suggest that this set of prayers belongs rather to the Ember season of December. A further point which would support such a theory is the content of the Proper Preface 434. The thought of the formula is directed towards true peace, concord, and charity:

> Vere dignum: qui fideles tuos mutua faciens lege concordes, veram pacem tuam tali foedere nexuisti, ut nec alteri quisquam moliretur infligere, quod sibi nollet inferri . . .

It seems likely then that both these formulae (433, 434) from set iv are equally well suited to a place in the liturgical year which has the Christmas festival in mind. Because this one set may possibly be placed more properly in the month of December it is nevertheless difficult to see why the rest of the sets in the group should be placed in that context merely on the basis of this one set of Mass prayers, as Bourque seems to do. Furthermore there seems to be no real reason why this should be necessary, unless it is first accepted that the 'libelli' of each group are conceived as a unit and thus the clue to the proper position

---

[1] Leo, *Sermones*, xvi and xvii (Migne, *P.L.* 54. 177–80).

of the whole group in the liturgical year is provided by this one set.

This collection of ORATIONES ET PRAECES DIURNAE contains many references to personal enemies (cf. 416, 419, 420, 428, 456, 530) chiefly to be found in the Proper Prefaces. It is of interest to note that out of the eighteen prefaces contained in this section only three appear to any great extent in other extant liturgical books.[1] Three others appear once in three separate extant manuscripts.[2] A further feature of the sets of formulae is the placing of some remarkably short, epigrammatic, terse collects alongside some of the longest and most involved prefaces in the whole Sacramentary. Muratori, commenting upon this section, remarks that no pope in his right mind would have finally published or approved of a Sacramentary that contains such prolix and undignified allusions to personal enemies; for this, as well as for other reasons, he considers the Leonianum to be merely a notebook preliminary to an authentic Sacramentary, which perhaps was never published after all; at the same time a large number of the less offensive forms are to be found in other extant liturgical books.

As in the section relating to civil strife and war the lack of detailed information in the formulae themselves had given rise to a number of alternative suggestions, so in this collection of formulae concerning internal conflict in the Church the same lack of detail is an obstacle to a definite date. Again Duchesne's warning must be heeded, namely that it is impossible to suggest a date quite unequivocally for this material; at the same time the circumstances surrounding one particular disruption within the Church seem to be more in keeping with our formulae than others and it is to this that our attention must now be turned. Muratori,[3] followed by Probst,[4] suggested one of the following three schisms: 1. Ursinus and Damasus (A.D. 366–7); 2. Eulalius and Boniface I (A.D. 419); 3. Bassus and Sixtus III (A.D. 433). This last can be discarded at once. The history of the accusations made by Bassus Patricius against Sixtus III, recounted by the *Liber Pontificalis*, is a pure adoption of the Symmachian apocryphal 'Gesta de Xysti purgatione' and bears no resemblance

---

[1] Formulae 434, 446, and 465.   [2] Formulae 458, 471, and 489.
[3] L. A. Muratori, *Liturgia Romana Vetus*, pp. 22–4.
[4] F. Probst, *Die ältesten römischen Sakramentarien und Ordines*, pp. 62–76, 104–9.

whatever to the truth of the matter.[1] The account which the *Liber Pontificalis* gives of the schism of Eulalius is also strongly romanticized, under the influence of the Symmachian apocryphal stories. The Eulalian schism lasted between three and four months (from 21 December A.D. 418 to 8 April 419) and not seven months and fifteen days.[2] The schism of Ursinus must be rejected for the same reason; Ursinus, elected 25 September 366, was banished from Rome in October of the same year. Duchesne[3] suggests that the siege of the basilica of Liberius, which ended with the defection of the Ursinian priests, is to be dated 26 October A.D. 366, when Ursinus was already in exile. However, he returned to Rome on 15 September of the following year and was expelled yet again—on this occasion for good—some two months later on 16 November. The revolt of the clergy against Zosimus continued and the Ballerini suggest that it is to this period of strife that these references should be attached. But in fact there was no declaration of a revolt—there is only proof of divisions, and of complaints sent to the court at Ravenna, for which the legates brought upon themselves the sentence of excommunication.[4] This was at the beginning of October. A little later Zosimus became gravely ill and from this illness he never recovered.

From the account given in the *Liber Pontificalis* of the pontificate of Symmachus it is quite evident that for some length of time, from the election itself (A.D. 498) to A.D. 506, the Christian community in Rome underwent a period of considerable turmoil and severe strife. In the first period (22 November A.D. 498–1 March A.D. 499) the quarrels were less ardent and

---

[1] Cf. Duchesne, *Lib. Pont.* i. cxxvi–cxxvii. The 'Gesta de Xysti purgatione' was composed about the year A.D. 501, the period when the 'Gesta Liberii', the legend about Pope Liberius, was also invented. The story was obviously invented by someone who wished to create a precedent for the trial of Pope Symmachus by a Council of the Church under the direction of Theodoric.

[2] Cf. Duchesne, *Lib. Pont.* i. 228 nn. 1 and 2; Jaffé, *Regesta Pontificum Romanorum*, i. 51–3. The funeral ceremonies of Zosimus, who died 26 December A.D. 418, had not even ended when Eulalius took over the Lateran basilica and had himself elected by a group of his partisans. Both parties held ordination services on Sunday, 29 December A.D. 418, Eulalius and his followers in the Lateran, the Bishop of Ostia having been brought from his sick bed to perform the ceremony, Boniface in another church with nine other bishops present.

[3] Duchesne, *Histoire ancienne de l'Église*, 2 (1907), pp. 455–61.

[4] P. Jaffé, op. cit. i. 345; a letter dated 3 October A.D. 418. Cf. also Duchesne, *Histoire ancienne de l'Église*, 3 (1907), p. 247.

the recognition of the election was only a prelude to the preparation for an all-out campaign during the second period against Symmachus. Clearly, during the second period the 'rally-cry' of the Laurentians is that Symmachus is an unworthy successor to the apostolic throne, because of his alleged depraved morality and his simony. Symmachus, a native of Sardinia, had been appointed Pope by the majority to oppose the concessions to the Emperor and the patriarch of Constantinople advocated by the party of his predecessor, Anastasius III, which elected him against the archpriest, Laurentius. In the year A.D. 498 Laurentius was acclaimed at St. Mary's basilica by a party of the clergy and by the majority of the Senate as the successor to Anastasius. Meanwhile, however, Symmachus had been chosen in the Lateran basilica. Because of the confusion which ensued, both parties finally agreed to have the dispute settled by Theodoric the Ostrogoth, who was at Ravenna. Accordingly deputations were sent and Theodoric finally accepted Symmachus as the lawful pope. However, as soon as he returned to Rome a council was summoned and met on 1 March A.D. 499, at which it was decided that no one had the right, neither the living pope nor anyone else, to concern himself about the election of a successor and to seek to form a party with a view to election. It is recorded that Laurentius took part in this council and subscribed to its statements, under his title as archpriest of St. Praxed.[1] A little later he became Bishop of Nucerina in Campania.

During the period after the election of the two rival candidates to the see of Peter, and before the judgement of Theodoric, it was almost inevitable that such opposing factions came to be expressed in more violent ways, in the forms of open aggression, riot, and bloodshed.[2] In spite of the judgement of Theodoric four troubled years ensued. Each of the factions stood fast, but that of Symmachus seemed to emerge badly from the struggle. The Senate, prompted by Festus and Probinus, was against him. Symmachus was driven to a final stand in St. Peter's; Laurentius having gained the support and occupied the other city and suburban churches—'solus autem Faustus exconsul

---

[1] 'Coelius Laurentius archipresbyter tituli sanctae Praxedis'.
[2] All the complaints are indicated in the Laurentian texts of the *Liber Pontificalis*. Naturally the Symmachian texts remain silent.

pro ecclesia pugnabat'[1] writes the melancholy author of the Symmachian *Liber Pontificalis*. It is also during these years, profiting from his position and hence his power, that Laurentius had his portrait placed among those of the legitimate popes along the gallery of the basilica of St. Paul's outside the Walls. Since the methods of violence did not seem to produce the desired results, a struggle of the pen ensued—pamphlets, chronicles, and a whole series of apocryphal stories were produced. On these grounds Symmachus decidedly had the advantage. It must be noted, however, that the antagonists of Symmachus were men worthy of respect. The senators Festus and Probinus, the two chief leaders of the Laurentian faction, are also praised for their virtue and learning by Ennodius.[2] Laurentius himself is regarded for his austerity: 'in praediis memorati patricii Festi sine dilatione concessit, ibique sub ingenti abstinentia terminum vitae sortitus est.'

It is suggested that it is to this distressing and troubled situation that our formulae bear some relation. Symmachus, trusting in the Divine providence and bearing high office in the Church, earnestly desires the courts of the celestial city:

. . . qui in tua protectione confidunt, ut te solo praesule gloriantes tuo semper foveantur auxilio: per. (526.)

fac nos atria supernae civitatis et te inspirante semper ambire. (550.)

It is clear that he is uneasy in his mind in view of the prevailing strife:

Deus, qui prudentem sinceramque concordiam tuorum cordibus inesse voluisti, da nobis legitimae dilectionis tenere mensuram, ut qui a iuste (pacis puritate) dissentiunt, in nobis tamen, quod merito debeant lacerare, non habeant: per. (420.)

Adesto nobis, omnipotens et misericors deus, et sacramenta quae sumpsimus, nec nostris excessibus, nec alienis nos permittas violari peccatis: per. (519.)

. . . sed potius amare concedas qui veraciter arguunt, quam qui fallaciter blandiuntur: per. (438.)

The Pope meanwhile lost much patience and violently attacked

---

[1] Duchesne, *Lib. Pont.* i. 261.

[2] Magni Felicis Ennodii *Opera Omnia*, C.S.E.L. 6 (1882), pp. 401–10.

those who were leading the Church into such troubled times—
he openly enumerated their several misdeeds:

Vere dignum: qui caelestibus disciplinis ex omni parte nos instru-
ens, qualiter a fidelibus tuis falsos fratres discerneremus ostendis
unigeniti tua voce pronuntias: ex fructibus eorum cognoscetis eos . . .
(530.)

. . . de his sunt enim inflati sensu carnis suae, et non tenentes caput . . .

This, it is suggested, is a reference to the arrogant and ambitious
who aspire, either for themselves or for their friends, to the chair
of Peter; this reproach of ambition and pride is renewed in the
Mass iii,

tumentium voluntatum respuamus adflatus (426);

and in the Mass xxii,

sicut superbis in sua virtute praesumentibus semper obsistis (540).

To continue with the preface 530,

. . . de his sunt, qui terrena sapientes ideo depraecantium te verba
fastidunt, quia animales atque carnalis, quae sunt spiritus dei,
stulta mente non capiunt . . .,

the pious adversaries of Symmachus are here envisaged: the
ascetic Laurentius, the impressive Paschasius, or the virtuous
senators Festus and Probinus. Indeed the Laurentian party was
much strengthened by the presence of the deacon Paschasius,
whose saintly reputation gave him great influence over his
people. Honoured as a saint and confessor in the Roman martyrology, Paschasius is said by Gregory the Great,[1] who highly
commends him for his sanctity and his orthodox writings, to
have persisted in his adherence to the Laurentian party until
the day of his death. The opening of this preface has already
pointed to the 'falsi fratres', who have too high a reputation
concerning themselves, but warned that they must not be
judged before their actions. The preface of Mass iii with the
same idea and in a similar tone clearly proclaims:

Nec eos fulcit aut munit, quia, ut se velare contendant, volumina
divina percurrunt . . . (428.)

---

[1] 'Mirae sanctitatis vir, eleemosynarum maxime operibus vacans, cultor paupe-
rum et contemplator sui' (Gregory I, *Dialogues* iv and xlii (Migne, *P.L.* 77. 396–7)).

The preface 530 continues in its condemnations:

... de his sunt reprobi circa fidem, quam, nescientes quae loquantur neque de quibus adfirment, sepe subvertere conati sunt et conantur ...

Those who were contending against the faith and had wanted the pope to be judged by a council had approved the intervention of Theodoric. It was those who previously had circulated information the truth of which was entirely without foundation; this, however, had later developed into a movement whose chief aim was to stir up ferment and disorder within the Church.

... De his sunt subdoli operarii, qui introeunt explorare aeclesiae libertatem quam habet in Christo, ut eam secum in turpem redigant servitutem ...

The senators Festus and Probinus were on good terms with Theodoric, so too was their candidate Laurentius, whereas Faustus and Symmachus were often unfavourably looked upon at court. The reproach of dubious plots to bring the Church under the subjection of the heretics enjoying the royal patronage is easily explained; it is a theme taken up in Masses i and xviii also. The Roman senate was only too pleased to have the opportunity to become embroiled in ecclesiastical affairs.

... De his sunt, qui penetrant domos, et captivas ducunt mulierculas, honeratas peccatis, non solum viduarum facultates, sed devorantes etiam maritarum ...

Clearly this ecclesiastical quarrel was having a widespread effect among the populace of Rome; it was also an embarrassment to Theodoric, who was at Ravenna. In the year A.D. 501, according to the ancient custom of the Roman Church, Symmachus had celebrated the feast of Easter on 25 March. Theodoric was only too pleased to seize this opportunity of summoning Symmachus to Ravenna. Symmachus set out and, having reached Rimini, he received the order for his arrest. When walking by the side of the sea on one occasion he noticed the women with whom he was supposed to have been living immorally passing by on their way to Ravenna. He realized that the question of the date of Easter was being used as a means of removing him from the city of Rome. That same night he escaped and made his way back to the city. In retaliation Theodoric appointed a legate who was to take charge of the See of Rome until the dispute between Laurentius and Symmachus ceased. This last measure was particularly grave—it more or less said that the chair of Peter was vacant and denied that there was a legitimate bishop of Rome. The person chosen as legate to the Roman See was a certain Peter, Bishop of Altinum, who made the situation worse by being obstinate and celebrating the feast of Easter anew on 22 April, as if it had never been celebrated on the 25 March. Symmachus protested about this intrusion, but no attention was paid to his objection. All the religious buildings of Rome with the exception of St. Peter's and all the goods of the church passed into the hands of the legate. As well as denouncing the ex-consuls Festus ('caput senatus') and Probinus, who had profited by enriching themselves at the expense of widows and orphans, Symmachus criticized the procedure of surrounding the houses of the women with whom he was supposed to have been living immorally in order to take them by force; eventually, however, these same women were destined to witness against him. The 'Christum in cubile requirentes'[1] of the preface of Mass iii must without doubt be explained in the same manner. Festus and Probinus supposed themselves to be working for the good of the Church. This proper preface (530) abounds in phrases reminiscent of certain parts of the New Testament, though not always directly quoted (cf. 1 Tim. 1: 7–8, 2 Tim. 2: 6–7, 5–6, 9). It is not just a matter of the author's literary style that such allusions have been made, but they are present to lend a certain directness and authority to the argument. The preface goes on to suggest further crimes and contention:

Isti iam nec iustos appetunt se videri, nec saltim deforis sunt vel dealbati vel loti, sed palam pudore calcato de pravis conversationibus suis etiam gloriantur . . . Nam cum in his quae videntur obscura sint et malae famae nigra dedecore, satis evidenter apparet haec eos in occulto gerere, quae etiam turpe sit dicere.

Under the phrases 'pravae conversationis, pudore calcato' is

[1] Cf. P. Batiffol, 'Christum in cubile', *Revue biblique*, 3 (1894), pp. 437–8; van Kosteren, 'Christum in cubile', *Revue biblique*, 4 (1895), pp. 65–6.

there not an allusion to certain of the incidents recounted by the Symmachian *Liber Pontificalis*:

etiam et sanctimoniales mulieres et virgines deponentes de monasteria vel de habitaculis suis, denudantes sexum femineum, caedibus plagarum adflictas vulnerabantur . . . ?[1]

Duchesne[2] sees in the words

isti non solum ad tuam gratiam venientes sui foeditate deterrent, sed etiam intrinsecus fratribus constitutis, pro quibus Christus est mortuus, offendiculum suae perversitatis opponunt . . .

a similar purpose to that which he supposes to be contained in the April Masses, namely a long diatribe against monks. But there is no question here at all of monks or of ascetics of any kind. The expression 'venientes ad tuam gratiam' need not necessarily be applied to 'the pagans who turn away from baptism'; it could equally well apply to heretics and to Arians in particular, openly tolerated at Rome during this time. But such prolonged attacks as we have seen in this preface are rare. Symmachus pities himself for the intrigues of which he is the unfortunate victim:

Maiestatem tuam, domine, supplices exoramus, ut nec terreri nos lacerationibus patiaris iniustis . . . (438.)

Conprime, domine, quaesumus, deus, iniqua loquentium, et eos qui nos muliuntur insimulare confuta: per. (456.)

. . . ut non tam nos exagitet inepta laceratio supervorum, quam potius moveat miseratio lacerantum. (458.)

Concede nobis, domine, veniam delictorum, et eos qui nos inpugnare moliuntur expugna: quia sub tuo munimine constitutis nulla diaboli nocevit obreptio: per. (533.)

More often, however, Symmachus, conscious of his role and of the perilous situation, speaks of prudence to avoid the snares into which it is so easy to fall and exhorts his followers to charity and justice (cf. Masses iv, xiv, xxiii, xlv). In this context Masses i and v are particularly noteworthy, each with its characteristic long preface. In the preface of the first set (416) the following expression is to be particularly noted: 'tu etenim, domine, mittens in medium nos luporum'. A very similar phrase is to be

---

[1] Duchesne, *Lib. Pont.* i. 261.
[2] Duchesne, *Histoire ancienne de l'Église*, 3 (1907), p. 143.

found in an inscription of Symmachus in the (circular) church of St. Andrew at the Vatican, probably placed there at the time when the schism was coming to an end:

> Simmacus has arces cultu meliore novavit
> Marmoribus titulis nobilitate fide.
> Nil formido valet. Morsus cessare luporum:
> Pastoris proprium continet aula gregem.

Theodoric, desirous of ending the schism as soon as possible, called together a number of the Italian bishops who were to meet in Rome and come to a decision about the Pope. Many of the bishops were hesitant at first and informed Theodoric accordingly; others more troubled at the gravity of the accusations made against Symmachus and the unhappy state of the church decided to act without delay. In May A.D. 501 the council assembled in the basilica of Julius (St. Mary in Trastevere), the most influential members being the metropolitan bishops of Milan, Ravenna, and Aquileia—Laurence, Peter, and Marcellinus—all of whom were favourable to Symmachus, the legitimate pontiff. The second session (not long after the first, there is no precise date given) was held in the church of S. Croce in Jerusalem in the Sessorian Palace. In order to reach this building from the Vatican the Pope (Symmachus) was obliged to walk across the city. On the way he and the clergy who were accompanying him were attacked, some of them wounded, and two of his priests killed. When he returned to the Vatican, it was impossible for him to leave, but meanwhile the council had begun its deliberations. Many things contributed to make the situation terribly involved. Some of the bishops, discouraged, considered their presence useless and departed. Theodoric, however, congratulated those who had persevered and finally the council got under way. Three officers were appointed to give Symmachus safe conduct, but, being obstinate, he refused to attend. Four successive delegations were sent to him and to each he gave the same reply, declaring that he and his priests had been cruelly treated. At length a last meeting took place on 23 October A.D. 501. The bishops issued a decree in which it was stated that Symmachus could not be judged for the crimes attributed to him and that he was ultimately answerable to the judgement of God; he could not be held culpable and therefore he must be recognized as the legitimate pontiff. His authority was restored and the churches given back. The faithful were constrained to obey him and the clergy were to be reconciled with him, otherwise they would be considered as heretics and schismatics. No sentence was passed on Peter of Altinum, who throughout the affair had been acting on orders from the king. Finally, in the year 507 Theodoric, who throughout the struggle had been opposed to Symmachus, became favourable to the legitimate pontiff. This change was the work of the Alexandrine deacon Dioscurus.

There is no improbability in attributing the composition of the sets of formulae under discussion to Symmachus himself, since we know that he worked in the field of liturgy. The contemporary witness of the *Liber Pontificalis* provides the information that he extended the use of the 'Gloria in Excelsis' in the episcopal Mass on Sundays and feasts of Martyrs.[1] John, the chief chanter, attributes to him a further important role:

post tunc [Gelasius] Simachus papa similiter et ipse annalem suum cantum ededit.

In view of the similarity, sometimes very striking, between the events and circumstances of the Laurentian schism, as it has been described above, and the contents of the formulae under discussion, it seems not unreasonable to conclude that this is the period to which our formulae must be assigned. In this section of the Sacramentary we come close to some of the original formulae, if not to the originals themselves, for many of them lack the polish and structure which liturgical prayer gradually developed; also outstanding is the obviously personal touch behind the prayer, of someone who is really within the 'Sitz im Leben'. Previously it has been stated that the formulae cannot be attached to a particular period in the Church's history with absolute certainty because of the lack of precise references within the formulae themselves, but nevertheless this does not prevent investigation and suggestion. Along with Bourque it is suggested that the period envisaged by these sets of Mass prayers in the Leonianum is the second phase of the Laurentian schism, and that they are to be dated about the years A.D. 500 to 506. If this is so, then their place of origin must undoubtedly be Rome.

[1] Duchesne, *Lib. Pont.* i. 263.

7

THE DATE OF THREE GROUPS
OF PRAYERS

I. *Group XXIX*: In Natale Episcoporum

As has already been pointed out in the general description
of the Sacramentary the title 'In Natale Episcoporum'
would seem to suggest that the whole group is related to
this particular topic. In fact it can be said that sets i–vii only
make reference to the anniversary of an episcopal consecration.
Set viii, though it contains the title PRO EPISC OFFERENDUM
before a proper 'Hanc igitur' prayer for insertion into the Canon
of the Mass, cannot be said to relate directly to the subject of an
episcopal consecration. Set v is a collection of nine collects and,
unlike the other sets, does not contain any other variable parts
of the Mass.

It was H. Lietzmann[1] who suggested that the first anniversary of the consecration of Pope Vigilius (29 March A.D. 538)
is that commemorated in the fourth set (983–8). Since both he
and Duchesne[2] favour the suggestion that this and the other
sets (i–vii) of this particular group are to be ascribed to the
pontificate of Vigilius, we must now go on to examine this
assertion more closely.

If several expressions which are used in the fourth set of
formulae are examined carefully, it can be concluded that this
set was used for a Mass which was celebrated a short time before
Easter, during the fast which preceded that great feast-day.
The actual day of Pope Vigilius' consecration was 29 March
A.D. 537, which in that year was the fifth Sunday in Lent. The
first anniversary of this day was observed a year later, but in
A.D. 538 29 March was Monday of Holy Week, and it is to

---

[1] H. Lietzmann, 'Petrus und Paulus in Rom', *Arbeiten zur Kirchengeschichte*, 1 (ed.
2, 1927), pp. 30–5; id., 'Zur Datierung des Sacramentarium Leonianum', *Jahrbuch
für Liturgiewissenschaft*, 2 (1922), pp. 101–2.

[2] L. Duchesne, *Origines du culte chrétien* (1925), pp. 372–81.

this day that Lietzmann would have us ascribe set iv of the consecration Masses. The text of the Gelasian Sacramentary (Vat. Reg. 316) presents the season of Lent as a 'paschal fast'.[1] This would accord with the evidence of the Leonianum, where such expressions are used which seem to indicate the imminence of Easter: 'ut ieiuniis paschalibus . . .' (984), 'et de congruo sacramenti pascalis' (987), 'et de sacrae festivitatis celebritate laetetur' (988). But this still does not afford any help in the way of fixing the occurrence of this set more precisely within the Lenten season.

During the fifth century there were four popes who were each consecrated in the month of March, and the claims of each of these to the paternity of these Masses must be examined. Pope Zosimus was consecrated 18 March A.D. 417 and died 26 December A.D. 418. He celebrated one anniversary only on the fourth Monday of Lent in A.D. 418. Pope Simplicius was consecrated 3 March A.D. 468 and died 10 March A.D. 483. The anniversaries of Simplicius' consecration were all celebrated in the Lenten season, between the first Monday and the third Saturday. Pope Felix III was consecrated 13 March A.D. 483 and died 11 March A.D. 492. He celebrated eight anniversaries, all of which fell between the first Wednesday and the fifth Monday of Lent. Pope Gelasius was consecrated 1 March A.D. 492 and died 21 November A.D. 496. His anniversaries occurred between the first Monday and the third Wednesday of Lent. However, nearer the feast of Easter itself there are two other names to be considered. Pope Vigilius was consecrated on 29 March A.D. 537 and Pope Pelagius I on 16 April A.D. 556. These are the only two popes who, before the seventh century, celebrated the anniversaries of their consecration during Holy Week. The anniversary of Vigilius fell on Monday in Holy Week in A.D. 538 and 549 (Wednesday in Holy Week in A.D. 541 and 552), and of Pelagius in A.D. 558 on the Tuesday of Holy Week. We have therefore six names, all of which may be considered to have a claim to the composition of these sets of Mass formulae. But for reasons which are now about to be put forward two names have been singled out for closer consideration, those of Vigilius and Pelagius. In what way therefore can

---

[1] Mohlberg, *Sacramentarium Gelasianum*, formula 94, 'Da quaesumus, domine, fidelibus tuis ieiuniis paschalibus . . .' and other similar phrases.

any definite conclusion be made in favour of one of these names? Chavasse[1] argues that the set vii of Mass formulae supposes the coincidence of the anniversary of that particular year with the feast of Easter (i.e. Easter Day and the eight days following). In this set of prayers there is no allusion to fasting; there is a reference to the Easter feast in the words 'pro reverentia paschali' (1004). The eight days of the octave are, he argues, an extension of the feast itself. The Gelasian Sacramentary (Vat. Reg. 316) employs similar expressions during the octave of Easter only— 'paschale mysterium recensentes', 'paschalibus gaudiis', etc.[2] Even if this fact allows us to dismiss all other popes except Vigilius and Pelagius, since their anniversaries all fall before Easter except in the case of the two in question, it still gives no further hint as to which of the two is the author. In A.D. 554 the anniversary of Pope Vigilius fell on the Tuesday in Easter Week and in A.D. 559 that of Pope Pelagius fell on the Wednesday in Easter Week. If the double allusion made concerning the apostle Paul by each of the Mass formulae (1004–5) was pressed as an indication of the place of a stational Mass, the balance would certainly be in favour of Pope Vigilius, since the station for the Tuesday in Easter Week is at St. Paul's whereas that for the Wednesday following Easter is at St. Laurence outside the Walls.

Chavasse argues in his article that the literary and the ideological characters of the seven sets of formulae both indicate that the name of Vigilius would not be out of keeping in regard to their authorship. But we must examine further the historical evidence concerning the number of anniversaries which were celebrated by each pope. Pelagius I celebrated his consecration anniversary on four occasions in Rome:

A.D. 557	3rd Monday after Easter
558	Tuesday in Holy Week
559	Wednesday after Easter
560	Friday after Easter

Pope Vigilius should have celebrated the anniversary of his consecration on many more occasions in Rome, but through force

---

[1] A. Chavasse, 'Messes du Pape Vigile dans le sacramentaire léonien', *Ephem. Lit.* 64 (1950), pp. 161–213; 66 (1952), pp. 145–219. Much of what now follows in the text is a presentation of the arguments of Chavasse and an assessment of them.

[2] Mohlberg, *Sacramentarium Gelasianum*, formulae 468, 469.

of circumstance he was able to celebrate the occasion eight
times only in Rome, between the years A.D. 538 and 545:

A.D. 538	Monday in Holy Week
539	3rd Tuesday in Lent
540	5th Thursday in Lent
541	Good Friday
542	3rd Saturday in Lent
543	6th Sunday in Lent (Palm Sunday)
544	Tuesday in Easter Week
545	4th Wednesday in Lent

On 22 November A.D. 545 Vigilius suddenly left Rome for
Constantinople, having been summoned by the emperor Justinian. Justinian had issued an edict against the writings of
Theodore of Mopsuestia and Theodoret, with which Vigilius
had refused to comply, seeing it as a rejection of the Chalcedonian theology. He never returned to his episcopal city; in fact
on his way back to Rome he died at Syracuse on 7 June A.D. 555.

A difficulty arises, however, over the fact that there are eight
anniversaries celebrated by Pope Vigilius and yet in the Leonianum there are seven sets of formulae only. Chavasse makes two
suggestions which provide possible solutions to this problem:
(*a*) In A.D. 541 the anniversary fell on Good Friday, a day when
there would be no possibility of celebrating his consecration,
though at the same time it must be suggested that at least one
prayer to this effect could have been inserted into the Synaxis
of the day. This really anticipates the next point, (*b*), that set v
really contains two separate sets of formulae of four and five
respectively: $v(a) = 989–92$; $v(b) = 993–7$. This then provides
a further set of formulae and makes up the corresponding
number of sets to the anniversaries celebrated by Vigilius. Two
further points are to be considered below which, Chavasse
argues, provide the necessary information for the ascription of
these sets i–vii to Pope Vigilius: (*a*) the order of the sets; (*b*) the
style and historical occasion, in so far as these can be determined
by such brief references.

Chavasse concludes that the allusions to events which are
made in the various formulae indicate the following order:
iv (A.D. 538), i (A.D. 539), ii (A.D. 540), iii (A.D. 543), vii (A.D.
544), but the place of the formulae $v(a)$, $v(b)$, and vi seems to

G

present some difficulty, so far as attributing them to a particular year is concerned. It has already been shown why iv and vii have been placed in A.D. 538 and A.D. 544 respectively. Set iii is ascribed to the year A.D. 543 (6th Sunday in Lent). In this set allusion is made to penitence:

ut declinemus noxios . . . respuamus.   (977.)
ut aeclesiae tuae praeces . . . fiant . . . gratiores.   (979.)

Prayer is also offered for the preservation of the Roman people from all attack:

ut tuae pacis abundantia . . . cumulentur.   (974.)
et nos a totius . . . custodis.   (975.)
quia tunc . . . internos.   (977.)

These are taken to be allusions to the campaign of Totila in A.D. 542–3. Totila, then ruler of Umbria, had himself by this time penetrated Tuscany, passed the Tiber, and come very near to the territory of Rome itself. The siege of Naples was begun in the autumn of A.D. 542 and by the spring of A.D. 543 the city had been taken. The plague of A.D. 542–3 is also mentioned in two indirect allusions, 'mortalitatis conscientia trepidos' (972, cf. also 990). The year A.D. 540 is chosen as that which is most fitting for the set ii. Allusion is made to penitence:

ut ab inprobis voluntatibus . . . correctis (966);

and the success of the Roman armies is besought:

da aeclesiae tuae pacem . . .   (963.)
Omnipotens sempiterne deus . . . possimus per.   (965.)

It was during this period that Vitiges had attacked Ravenna— the siege had commenced in the winter 539/40 and the city finally yielded in May 540. Chavasse considers the key phrase to set i is that which appears in formula 960:

securitas nobis . . . integritas.

This he considers to be an indirect allusion to the terrible siege of Milan by the Goths in the winter A.D. 538/9, when the city was destroyed and the inhabitants massacred and ill-treated.

Because of the recurrence of a doublet in the formula 990 (cf. 972) it is suggested that the whole of v(*a*) be placed in the year 542, at the beginning of the great plague. The station for the Wednesday in the fourth week of Lent is at St. Paul's, being placed at that church both by the Roman Epistle-list of Wurz-burg and in the 'Hadrianum',[1] from which it has found its way into the present-day Missale Romanum. There is a fleeting hint of 2 Cor. 12: 9 in formula 1000, and it is perhaps worthy of note also that the first formula of this set vi (998), 'Deus qui propter aeclesiae . . . non deseras', recalls the preface (374) of set xxvi of group XV (IN N APOSTOLORUM PETRI ET PAULI). It is upon this evidence that this particular set is ascribed to the year A.D. 545. It only remains now that the set v(*b*) should be placed in the year 541, since this is the only remaining combination possible. The result of this study in tabular form, following Chavasse, would appear as follows:

Sets of formulae	29 March	Year	Easter
i	3rd Tuesday in Lent	539	26 April
— (v(*a*))	3rd Saturday in Lent	542	20 April
— (vi)	4th Wednesday in Lent	545	16 April
ii	5th Thursday in Lent	540	8 April
iii	6th Sunday in Lent	543	5 April
iv	Monday of Holy Week	538	4 April
v(*a*)	—	—	—
v(*b*)	Good Friday	541	31 March
vi	—	—	—
vii	Tuesday after Easter	544	27 March

In support of certain of the suggestions made above it is evident that some of the formulae suggest that the bishop whose conse-cration they commemorate has not been very long in his office: 'suscepta principia' (986), 'sumpta primordia', 'tuis principiis' (955). Again, on the other hand, there are some which suggest the opposite: 'sicut de initiis tuae gratiae gloriamur, ita de perfectione gaudere' (1006), 'cum accessu temporum' (1001). It is further suggested that the occurrence of two identical prayers in the sets iii and v(*a*) (972 and 990), each with an allusion to the plague (*mortalitas*), explains perhaps that the two sets

---

[1] Cf. *The Gregorian Sacramentary*, ed. Wilson, p. 40.

pertain to two consecutive years (A.D. 542–3). It was at this time that the plague was particularly bad in Italy. The allusions to fasting and the observance of the commandments which are found in certain of the sets are no doubt explained by their coincidence with the Lenten fast (vi—538, ii—540, v(b)—541, and iii—543).

It would be true to say that with the exception of set v all the sets have the same construction in the last three formulae, namely a proper preface followed by two post-communion prayers. Sets vi and viii are similar in that each of them contains two collects, a proper preface, and two post-communion prayers, which is certainly true of a large number of other sets within the Leonianum. Six formulae appear before the proper preface in the second set and three formulae in a similar position in the fourth set. The fifth set is a collection of nine formulae which appear to be collects only. In addition to two formulae and a proper preface, there is a proper 'hanc igitur' and 'quam oblationem' in the first set; these are followed by two post-communion formulae. The third set, in the actual number of formulae it contains, is the largest of the group. A proper 'memento' is preceded by five formulae and is followed by a further three prayers, a proper preface, and two post-communion prayers.

The set v(b) has been placed in the year 541 when the celebration that year occurred on Good Friday; hence, Chavasse argues, there are no other Mass prayers except the five collects which could be used during the Synaxis proper to that day. But similarly we are left with four collects in the set v(a) which could equally well be used during the course of the Good Friday Synaxis. The only reason why the year 542 is chosen as appropriate is that a similar reference, indeed the same formula which contains this reference, appears in set iii, which has been placed in the year 543; both then cover the plague years A.D. 542 and 543. If, however, we are to divide any set of formulae, a step which in itself seems questionable, then set iii is suggested as being the most appropriate. Why divide set v at all? It is quite possible that from the nine formulae contained therein one or more could have been used at the Synaxis of the day in A.D. 542. With the division of set iii the first part consists of formulae 971–7 and the second 978–82. The second section would thus be in harmony with a pattern already found in sections vi and vii—

namely, a collect, a secret prayer, a proper preface, and two post-communion prayers. If this plan were to be adopted, then some slight alteration in the relation of the various sets to their respective years would have to be made. If the set v is not divided but remains as suggested a complete set, then the whole of the set would be placed in the year 541, when the anniversary fell on Good Friday. The set iii(*a*), which contains the veiled reference to the plague, could remain in the year 543 (as Chavasse suggests) and the set iii(*b*) would have to be placed in the year 542, since that is the only possible alternative.

But it is difficult to accept the dating of a number of these sets in so precise a manner in view of the scant references provided by the text. It would perhaps be true to say that the ascription of sets iv and vii to the years 538 and 544 respectively is based on evidence which seems much more reliable than that which is used to justify the date given to the other sets within this group. As Duchesne so rightly points out in respect of the Vitiges Mass,[1] particular conclusions must not be sought from general references, for often such references are so vague that it is impossible to state unequivocally that they belong to one particular date. It is precisely this situation which arises in the attempt to systematize the sets here in question. Bourque,[2] from an examination of the evidence contained in sets iv and vii, for these are the most important in respect of their content for the dating, prefers the pontificate of Pelagius I, who in A.D. 558 celebrated his anniversary in Holy Week. The set iv, which clearly belongs to Holy Week, has no reference to the state of war and turmoil or of the deliverance which Rome accepted in that year with great relief; hence Bourque insists that this set cannot belong to the year 538 since it was at this time that the campaign of Vitiges was at its height and only just before Easter he had withdrawn from the siege of the city. Bourque considers that such a situation must have been reflected in the liturgy of the time. A.D. 558 is suggested as the year to which set vii properly belongs—again in the pontificate of Pelagius I. Bourque does not attempt to make any further suggestions regarding the dating of the other five sets. For this group of seven sets the date A.D. 557–60 is given.

---

[1] See above, p. 55.
[2] Bourque, op. cit., pp. 100–4.

The object of this short study has been to examine and comment upon the hypotheses presented which relate to the seven sets of formulae to be used on the occasion of an episcopal ordination. Having accepted Chavasse's suggestions that sets iv and vii be attributed to Vigilius rather than Pelagius, we must pay due attention also to Bourque's reluctance to fix a date to any of the other sets; hence the suggestion is that acceptance be given to A.D. 538–45 as the period within which these prayers are to be dated. Whether we accept Pelagius or Vigilius one point is certain—such phrases as

nec inferni portas apostolicae confessioni . . .   (975)

and

sedem tamen beati apostoli tui Petri . . .   (989)

point quite clearly to Rome as the place of origin of these formulae and the bishop of Rome whose celebration it is. As has happened with other prayers in the Leonianum a number of these have been reproduced with slight changes or omissions in the Gelasian Sacramentary (Vat. Reg. 316). The set in this book entitled 'Missa quam pro se episcopus die ordinationis suae cantat' contains no fewer than three of the Leonine prayers— 964 as a collect, 999 as a secret prayer, and 1007 as a postcommunion prayer. None of these formulae, however, finds a place in the present-day Missale Romanum.

II. *The Mass* In Dedicatione *in the Month of April*

Feltoe comments on the title of this Mass which is inserted in red in the margin: 'I am not sure that this marginal rubric is in the same hand as most of the other rubrics, though I am inclined to think so.'[1] He wrongly asserts that none of the formulae of this Mass occurs elsewhere. The text of the first formula (130), 'Deus, qui beati Petri apostoli . . . ', is found in three non-Roman sources with only very slight variations in the text. In the Missale Gothicum[2] it forms the collect for the feast of the Conversion of St. Paul and makes no mention of the apostle

---

[1] Feltoe, op. cit., p. 177 (note on p. 15, l. 13 IN DEDICATIONE).
[2] L. C. Mohlberg, *Missale Gothicum* (Cod. Vat. Reg. 317), Rerum Ecclesiasticarum Documenta, Series Maior, Fontes V, Rome, 1961, formula 143.

Peter at all. (The name Peter in our collect is replaced by that of Paul.) In the Rosslyn Missal the text appears under the heading IN COMMEMORATIONE S.S.P.(ETRI) ET P.(AULI) and, as the title indicates, both Peter and Paul are mentioned in the opening phrase.[1] The formula is also to be found in the Missale Drummondiense. Feltoe also suggests that the phrase in the secret prayer (131) 'cui haec est basilica sacrata' was meant to be used on the feast of the dedication of St. Peter's at Rome. It seems that such a phrase as 'ubi venerabiles eius reliquiae conquiescunt', which occurs in the Preface (132), might support such a theory.

This formula appears in the midst of a set of prayers which indicate their place of origin as Rome; the set itself is to be found in the opening section of the book, which has been described elsewhere as a Common of martyrs/confessors.[2] It is a set of Mass formulae composed for the dedication of a basilica which Bourque[3] suggests is not a city church of St. Peter, but a basilica outside the city. The prayers show that it is a basilica dedicated to St. Peter, but situated outside Rome and at a place where the apostle's relics are not preserved:

Vere dignum: qui ut in omni loco dominationis tuae beati Petri apostoli magnificis potestatem, non solum ubi venerabiles eius reliquiae conquiescunt, sed ubicumque praetiosa reverentia fuerit invocata, tribues esse praesentem . . . (132.)

The following collect also makes a similar allusion:

Deus, qui beati Petri apostoli dignitatem ubique facis esse gloriosam . . . (130.)

This would therefore exclude the two city churches in Rome itself, i.e. St. Peter ad Vincula, established in Rome in the fifth century, and the basilica on the Vatican. The *Liber Pontificalis* from the fifth to seventh centuries only mentions one basilica outside Rome dedicated to St. Peter and consecrated by the Pope. The event occurred during the pontificate of Symmachus (A.D. 498–514):

Item via Tribuna, miliario XXVII ab urbe Roma [beatus Symmachus] rogatus ab Albino et Glaphyra pp. inlustris, de proprio

---

[1] The Rosslyn Missal (ed. Lawlor, Henry Bradshaw Society), p. 83, l. 35.
[2] See below, pp. 103 and 133.   [3] Bourque, op. cit., pp. 141–3.

faciens a fundamento, basilicam beato Petro in fundum Pacinianum dedicavit.[1]

(Manuscripts B, C, D, G, of the *Liber Pontificalis* use the words 'Via Trivana' in this extract; many use the description 'Via Tiburtina'.) A road to Rome with the name Tribuna or Triviana does not exist. The Tiburtine Way must also be excluded because it extends only 20 miles from Rome. Duchesne thinks it must be the Tiberine Way, a road which branches off from the Via Flaminia at Saxa Rubra, whilst Mommsen prefers the Via Trivana.

Albinus, *praefectus praetorius*, Bourque suggests, is probably to be identified as the consul of A.D. 493 and the 'vir illustris' to whom many letters of Ennodius are addressed. The year of the dedication is not indicated, but it must have been after A.D. 506, i.e. the end of the Laurentian schism in Rome. The *Liber Pontificalis* clearly indicates this—after having mentioned the dissensions at the beginning of the pontificate of Symmachus it continues:

> Post haec omnia beatus Symmachus invenit manichaeos in urbe Roma . . .[2]

There then follows a list of churches and oratories founded during this time, among which this basilica of St. Peter is mentioned. It is a certain fact that the measures against the Manichaeans did not come into force until after A.D. 507. The date for the composition of this set of formulae can therefore be fixed at some time during the years A.D. 507 to 514, though a more precise date is impossible. The exact situation of the 'fundum Pacinianum' can never be known with absolute certainty. It is supposed to have been discovered at Cave, a village situated some 26 miles from Rome, near Tivoli; but others wish to place it near Vicavaro, the market town which today has the name Pacciano.

III. *The Feast of St. John the Baptist*

There are five sets of Mass formulae for this feast under the title VIII KAL IUL N SCI IOHANNIS BAPTISTAE. The fourth of these five sets bears the title AD FONTEM. It is worthy of note that all

---

[1] Duchesne, *Lib. Pont.* i. 263.   [2] Ibid. 261.

the formulae make effective use of the figure of new birth and the attainment of this state in baptism:

Annue, domine, praecibus nostris, ut sicut de praeteritis ad nova sumus sacramenta translati, ita vetustate deposita sanctificatis mentibus innovemur: per. (250.)

The second prayer of the set expresses similar thoughts:

Da, quaesumus, domine, lumen intellegentiae parvulis tuis, ut pro veteris gratia sacramenti praesentis sacrificii gratia succedente sic gloriemur nobis . . . (248.)

It is perhaps this aspect of the prayers which will allow their origin and date to be fixed. The Gregorian Sacramentary, which has strong connections with the Lateran basilica, gives an account of the Pope blessing the Holy Oils in that basilica on Maundy Thursday: 'Benedicit tam Domnus papa quam omnes presbyteri.'[1] On Holy Saturday the Pope comes to the Lateran baptistry for the last preparatory ceremonies of the catechumens after the 'traditio symboli': 'Ad reddentes dicit dominus papa. Post pisteugis (pospiteuis). Item ad catechizandos infantes.'[2] Each day during the octave of Easter a station was made at the same baptistry, 'ad fontes'.[3] In addition, on the feasts of John the Evangelist[4] and John the Baptist,[5] after whose names two oratories in the same basilica are dedicated, there is a station 'ad fontes'. The occurrence of this commemoration of baptism on the feast-day of these particular saints can only be explained by this local factor.

Bourque[6] suggests that the formulae here in question are papal in origin. The date must be after the pontificate of Hilary (A.D. 461–8) who, so the *Liber Pontificalis*[7] informs us, had the two subsidiary oratories built on to the Lateran basilica, the one bearing the name of the Evangelist, the other the name of the Baptist:

Hic (Hilarius) fecit oratoria tria in baptisterio basilicae Constantinianae, sancti Ioannis Baptistae, sancti Ioannis evangelistae et sanctae Crucis . . .

---

[1] *The Gregorian Sacramentary*, ed. Wilson, p. 49. [2] Ibid. p. 54.
[3] Ibid., pp. 60, 61, 62, 63, 64, 65 (twice).
[4] Ibid., p. 14. [5] Ibid., p. 85.
[6] Bourque, op. cit., pp. 114–15.
[7] Duchesne, *Lib. Pont.* i. 242, and note 3 on p. 245.

The dedicatory inscription of these chapels of the Lateran basilica reads:

Hilarius episcopus et sanctae plebi dei Liberatori suo beato Ioanni evangelistae Hilarius episcopus famulus xpi.

8

SOME THEOLOGICAL POINTS FROM
THE SACRAMENTARY

SINCE the Sacramentary is divided into so many groups,
each dealing with a particular topic in itself, and because
the work is a compilation from many sources, it is impossible to give an account of the theology of the Sacramentary
as such; also some groups are more fitting for such a discussion
than others. The following study therefore is based upon particular groups which form a distinct and convenient arrangement
for such a task; these are the sets of Mass formulae provided for
(I) an ordination, (II) Christmas, (III) Ascension and Pentecost, (IV) the Departed, and (V) the feast of SS. Peter and Paul.

I

The month of September makes provision for the consecration of a bishop, the ordination of a presbyter, and the making
of a deacon. The sets of formulae for each occasion are to be
found in group XXVIII, with the following titles and in the
following order: CONSECRATIO EPISCOPORUM, BENEDICTIO SUPER
DIACONOS, and CONSECRATIO PRESBYTERI. The first Roman rite of
ordination, indeed the earliest of them all, is that preserved in
the Apostolic Tradition of Hippolytus assigned to the early part
of the third century. In this document the actual ordination
prayer is preserved, as in the Leonianum, but in addition
various directions about the actions of those participating in the
rite are also given. The bishop who has previously been elected
by all the people has hands laid upon him by the other bishops
present. All are enjoined to 'keep silence praying in the heart
for the descent of the Holy Spirit'.[1] Then one of the bishops
present, at the request of all, lays hands upon him who is to be
consecrated and recites the prayer. The prayer over the bishop

[1] G. Dix, O.S.B. (ed.), *The Apostolic Tradition of Hippolytus* (London, 1937), p. 3.

recalls that God Himself instituted the princes and priests of old. Now the gift of the Spirit is besought for the bishop who is to serve as Christ's 'high priest'. The functions of the bishop are to forgive sins, assign lots (ordain), loose every bond, please God, and offer the gifts (celebrate the Eucharist).[1] It is quite clear in the prayer over the presbyter that the presbyterate is seen as a delegated office from the episcopate. The bishop is likened to Moses, who was commanded by God to choose presbyters. No mention is made of any specific duties assigned to the presbyter. The deacon, quite clearly, is 'not ordained for a priesthood, but for the service of the bishop that he may do the things commanded by him'.[2] It is evident from these prayers that the elected presbyter becomes a member of the sacerdotal body which, with the bishop, is responsible for the oversight of the faithful. The presbyter participates in the 'sacerdotium' of the bishop, whilst the deacon is ordained solely for the ministry of the bishop ('in ministerio episcopi'). The deacon does not receive the 'communem presbyteri spiritum' of which the presbyters are partakers. Thus in the Hippolytean rite the reference of the priesthood and the diaconate to the episcopate is quite clear. The bishop is the pastor and high priest and it is in his high-priesthood that the presbyterate shares, not only in the eucharistic context but also in the whole sphere of ecclesiastical government. Briefly, this is the only evidence we have of the ordination rite at Rome until three centuries later fresh evidence is encountered in the Leonianum; the ordination prayers of this book, Botte maintains, represent the 'pure Roman rite'.[3] Hence it is useful to have in mind the only other existing text of ordination prayers from Rome as it is presented in the Apostolic Tradition.

Unlike the evidence which appears in Hippolytus, where both the actual rite is described and the forms of prayer are given, in the Leonianum the forms of prayer only are to be found. The very order and title of these three sets of prayers give some indication of what we may expect; the consecration of the bishop appears first, followed by the 'blessing over the deacon'. The diaconate, it seems, is still conceived of as being a definite order (and not just a lower point in the ascent to the priesthood)

---

[1] Dix, op. cit., p. 5.　　　　　　　　[2] Ibid., p. 15.
[3] *The Sacrament of Holy Orders* (Eng. edn., London, 1962), p. 8.

and is still strongly attached to the personal service of the episcopate—a point which will be made in the prayer over the deacon at his ordination. There then follow the ordination prayers for the presbyter. In the titles for the bishop and presbyter the term 'consecratio' appears and indicates the particular act of ordination, whilst that used for the deacon is 'benedictio' which conveys the idea of 'set aside' rather than 'ordained' in the technical sense.

In the consecration prayer for a bishop (947) one single theme pervades the whole. The bishop is the high priest of the new dispensation—an idea which also finds its place in the Hippolytean prayer. Under the old dispensation Aaron had been appointed and ordained in two rites, one in which he was clothed with the garments appropriate to his office and the other in which he was anointed. This scheme is now applied to the high priest of the new dispensation and what happens to him at his 'consecratio'. The thought moves into the spiritual—the soul of the elect bishop is clothed in a more glorious fashion by the divine blessing and his whole being is pervaded by the unction of the Holy Spirit. Of course the vesting and unction became parts of the ordination rite in later ages, but it is highly unlikely that the passage is to be taken in a literal sense—it is purely symbolic at this stage. In any event such ceremonies when they were introduced into the Roman rite came from a non-Roman source. The typological approach which is to be found here is not unknown in other rites, especially some eastern liturgies, but it is in the Roman rite that it is so striking because it is so developed. In many ways it is with St. Cyprian that the first decisive development is made in the conception of the Christian ministry. According to the Cyprianic theory the Christian bishop was the equivalent of the Jewish high priest, and the presbyterate the Levitic tribe of the new dispensation. He does not hesitate to apply the Levitic directions to the Christian priesthood so that the injunction of Lev. 19: 32, that the people should rise at the entrance of the Levites, is interpreted quite literally of the Christian presbyterate.[1] It has been argued that the choice of the Aaron typology is to emphasize the ritual function of the bishop, but this seems unlikely; the real point is that it is the same Spirit which is being given in both the divine actions.

[1] Cf. Cyprian's designation of the presbyterate as the 'levitica tribus', *Ep.* i. 1.

The prayer for the ordination of a presbyter (954) can conveniently be divided into three sections. The first is the exordium 'Domine, sancte Pater. . .', which gives glory to God, the source and dispenser of all offices, through whom all things are established. The second section deals with the application of this to the old dispensation and the rise of priestly orders and levitical offices. Moses and the seventy elders, Aaron and his two sons are cited as particular examples. The prayer then goes on to mention the 'teachers of the faith' who were to share the apostolate of Jesus Christ. The last part contains a prayer to God, made by the bishop, who also has need of helpers. What we have already observed in the Hippolytean prayer is again evident from this text, namely that the presbyterate is very much a derived office from the episcopate: 'sequentis ordinis viros', 'secundae dignitatis', 'secundi meriti munus'. In the Leonine Sacramentary the work of the presbyter is somewhat more clearly defined than that of the bishop:

ut cum pontifices summos regendis populis praefecisses, ad eorum societatis et operis adiumentum sequentis ordinis viros et secundae dignitatis elegeris.

The prayer for the making of a deacon (951) opens in a similar way to that for the presbyter, in that it accords to God the glory for his providence in all things. He has himself organized the three orders of servants fighting for his name. Mention is again made of the Levites, and God is asked to send down His Holy Spirit so that the deacons might work in the fullness of the sevenfold gifts of the Spirit. The graces and virtues which should be theirs are enumerated so that they may be an example for the people to imitate.

Though no provision is made or instruction given concerning ritual action at an ordination, it is quite likely that this rite consisted of the laying-on of hands and prayer and that the prayer used is that which appears in the Leonianum for each of the several orders. A conception which is quite clear is that the structure of those offices in the church—bishop, deacon, and presbyter—is willed and created by God. In whatever way he may have been elected, it is really God who chooses the bishop, and it is this choice which is signified in the act of ordination. As the example given us by St. Cyprian shows, even though the people, the older clergy, and the other bishops have all voted, this is the 'judicium Dei'; now the bishop is responsible and answerable to God alone for his actions.[1] The bishop is clearly shown as the successor of the apostles; the gift of the Holy Spirit is for his aid in ruling the Church and the continuation of the apostolic work. It has been suggested above that the presbyter is subordinate to the bishop and in what way this is so; nevertheless he does participate in the priesthood of the bishop but at a lower level, so to speak. Whilst the presbyters are involved in the presbyterate of the bishop it is evident that the deacon is the servant of the bishop. During the liturgy he would no doubt act in his capacity as the bishop's personal assistant and perhaps the nearest parallel we have in modern times as regards his day-to-day duties, so far as the Church was concerned, is that of an archdeacon. The typology of these prayers is important in that it keeps in mind the working and power of God both under the old dispensation and its ordering, and now under the new. The new Israel of God, the Church, is ruled and governed by those endued with the same Spirit from on high. Although this is an investigation into the theology of the ordination prayers, a passing reference must be made to Wilson's[2] remarks that the CONSECRATIO EPISCOPORUM and the BENEDICTIO DIACONI are metrically regular throughout, that the CONSECRATIO PRESBYTERI is less so, and that this is taken by some as an indication that the formula has been worked over by a later hand. Rule[3] would support a theory of two such revisions. But in the absence of any clear evidence such suggestions must of necessity remain open.

II

The nine sets of prayers which serve for the feast of Christmas must now be examined, with regard to their theological content. One very marked feature which distinguishes this group from others in the Sacramentary is the occurrence of extensive quotations from Scripture in three of the proper prefaces. The texts

[1] Cyprian, *Ep.* lv. 21: '. . . actum suum disponit et dirigit unusquisque episcopatus, rationem propositi sui Domino redditurus.'
[2] H. A. Wilson, 'The Metrical Endings of the Leonine Sacramentary', *J.T.S.* 6 (1905), pp. 389–90.
[3] M. Rule, 'The Leonine Sacramentary: An analytical Study', *J.T.S.* 9 (1908), pp. 515–56; 10 (1909), pp. 54–99.

of Matt. 1: 23, John 1: 14, and Isa. 9: 6–7 are very familiar in the Christmas context:

> ... filium et vocamus nomen eius Emmanuhel et nobiscum deus est: quia verbum caro factum habitavit in nobis. Ecce puer natus est nobis, parvulus datus est nobis; et factus est principatus, cuius potestas super humeros eius; et vocabitur admirabilis, consiliarius, deus fortis, pater futuri saeculi, princeps pacis. Multiplicabitur eius imperium, et pacis non erit finis super solium David et super regnum eius, ut confirmet illud et corroboret amodo et usque in sempiternum ... (1245.)

An even greater multiplicity of Biblical texts proclaims the Christmas message with great exuberance in the third set:

> Vere dignum: hoc praesertim die, quo ipsum salutis nostrae sacramentum in lucem gentium revelasti, et ab uteri virginalis arcano ineffabili editione promisisti: erigens nobis cornum salutis in domo David pueri tui, ad dandam scientiam salutis populo tuo in remissionem peccatorum eorum, per viscera misericordiae tuae, in quibus visitavit nos oriens ex alto. Benedictus, qui venit in nomine domini; qui tamquam sponsus procedens de thalamo suo deus dominus et inluxit nobis, ut nos de tenebris et umbra mortis regnum perpetuae lucis [aeternae] efficeret ... (1247.)

In this short preface five quotations are from the New Testament (Luke 2: 32, Luke 1: 69, 77, 78, Matt. 4: 16) and three are taken from the Psalter (Pss. 118: 26, 19: 5, 118: 27).

Bourque[1] suggests that these sets are of papal origin and that the reference in formula 1268 indicates that the station was at S. Peter's, where the third Mass of Christmas was celebrated:

> Ut ad salutaris hodiernae generationis exordium pertinere mereamur, apostolicis tribue nos, domine, quaesumus, praecibus adiubari: per.

This group is particularly interesting for a study of the theological contents of the Sacramentary. Obviously, in the time of Christological debate one of the best occasions for a clear exposition would have been the Christmas feast, the celebration of the Incarnation, the fact that God was made man. Clear indications appear in our formulae which suggest that the

[1] Bourque, op. cit., pp. 128–9.

debate concerning the person of the Lord had not yet been settled. The proper preface, which opens

Vere dignum: ecce enim, sicut per os locutus est prophetarum ... (1245),

and contains the long extract from scripture quoted above, ends with the words:

In quibus omnibus evidenter deum hominemque cognoscimus, qui suscipiendo quod nostrum est, dignatus est nobis conferre quod suum est. Unde profusis gaudiis.

Passages in the *Sermons* of Pope Leo for the feast of the Nativity show very close similarity to the thought enshrined in this prayer. The person of the Incarnate Lord is described in this formula as 'deum hominemque', thus repudiating any Monophysite conception. A further and perhaps more pronounced statement is to be found in formula 1252:

Da, quaesumus, domine, populo tuo inviolabilem fidei firmitatem; ut qui unigenitum tuum in tua tecum gloria sempiternum in veritate nostri corporis natum de matre virgine confitentur, et a praesentibus liberentur adversis, et mansuris gaudiis inserantur: per.

The two natures of the Incarnate Christ again form a prominent part of the thought of this formula. It resembles the statement of Leo in the Tome where he writes:

idem vero sempiterni genitoris unigenitus sempiternus natus est de Spiritu sancto et Maria virgine.

The trend of Eutychianism was undoubtedly to deny the reality of the Lord's manhood and, in consequence, of his human body also. Indeed the more extreme Eutychians did assert, as some Apollinarians and Valentinians, that the Lord's body was not of the Virgin. These two extracts safeguard the orthodox teaching of Chalcedon and show close similarities of thought and expression to a number of the writings of Pope Leo, who played a leading role, though not actually present, in the formulations of the Chalcedonian Council.

The term 'sacramentum' appears in a number of formulae within the Christmas group—1328, 1305, 1262, and 1247. Its use is, however, not confined to this season. The formula 570 contains the phrase 'paschale sacramentum', which appears to be crucial for the dating of that particular set. Originally it meant the pledge or deposit in money which, in certain cases, according to Roman law, both plaintiff and defendant were expected to make; later it signified the military pledge and eventually it was applied to any oath whatever. In its use in the early Christian world it was applied to any sacred and solemn act or event. St. Cyprian uses the term 'sacramentum' in a wide variety of ways—for a mystery (*De Dom. Orat.* 9), a sacred symbol (*De Unit. Ecc.* 7), a sacred bond (*De Bap.* 7), and a sacred truth (*De Orat.* 28). Pope Leo employs this term frequently in his Sermons, again in a wide variety of meanings—mystery, sacred act, fact, rite, and meaning. It seems likely that in the text of the formulae above the term 'sacramentum' is used to indicate the mystery of the Incarnation and also implied is some idea of its solemn observance.

The present-day Roman Missal uses in the Mass rite the first prayer of the Christmas group,

Deus, qui humanae substantiae . . . (1239),

but since the prayer is said as the celebrant pours wine and water into the chalice, an extra clause has been added at this point to make the prayer more closely applicable to the action being performed. Thus 'per huius aquae et vini mysterium' is inserted between the words 'da nobis' and 'eius divinitatis'. As Jungmann[1] points out, it is in the eleventh century that 'the Christmas thought, which hardly ever came under discussion in this connection in the literature of the foregoing centuries, the thought of man's participation in the divinity through the Incarnation of the son of God, suddenly comes into prominence'. It is probably true to say that both the Eastern interpretation of the admixture rite, the divine and human natures of the Lord, and the Western interpretation, our own union with the Lord, are both to some extent reflected in this prayer. Certainly the theme of our own union with the Christ and his taking upon himself our nature is to be found in these formulae. The formula 1249 uses the phrase 'sacrosancta commercia' (cf. 1260), but this we also find in formula 555 used in the context of an Easter

---

[1] J. A. Jungmann, S.J., *The Mass of the Roman Rite* (American edn., New York, 1955), vol. 2, pp. 62–3.

Mass. Clearly the whole of the Christ event and its salvific power for mankind is envisaged in the use of such a term. God has wonderfully established the dignity of our human nature in his act of creation, but yet in the Incarnation of his son, who becomes man and knows all human weakness, pain, and suffering, he more wonderfully restores this same human nature. The Christ's participation in our manhood is seen as the assurance that the faithful believer will have fellowship within the Godhead. A passing reference must be made to the formula 1262, in which the celebrant inveighs against those who do not wish to believe the mystery of the Incarnation, which, he says, is shown forth in all the world:

Vere dignum: quoniam verae magnum, quod sine exemplo est singulare, quod sine humana ratiocinatione mirabile tuae pietatis editum sacramentum, adque ideo sicut primis fidelibus extitit in sui credulitate praetiosum, ita nunc excusabilem conscientiam non relinquit, quae salutaris mysterii veritatem toto etiam mundo testificante non sequitur . . .

Again the thought in this preface is not unlike that to be found in two of Leo's Sermons in which he exhorts the Christian people to share in the joy of the Christmas festival.[1]

III

The formulae within groups IX and X are concerned with the feasts of the Ascension and Pentecost respectively. There are a large number of proper prefaces in the former group, one of which (175) is reproduced to a large extent in the Missale Romanum in the proper preface for Ascension. The formulae strike an exultant note of joy that the Christ has now ascended into the heavens where he has entered upon his kingly reign in glory:

Vere dignum: quia mirantibus angelis angelorumque principibus rex gloriae dominusque virtutum resurrectionis beatae primitias, throno tuae maiestatis oblatus, in tua secum dextera collocavit. Et ideo. (177.)

Names given to the Christ in this group of formulae do not appear very regularly, if at all, in the rest of the Sacramentary: 'redemptor, mediator, auctor, rex gloriae': these all emphasize

---

[1] Leo, *Sermones*, xxi, xxii.

the significance of the work of the ascended Lord. A further theme of this group is the prayer that mankind may become sharers in that glorified human nature which the Ascension proclaims. The theme of section IV of Leo's *Sermon* (lxxiii. 1) is that the Ascension of Christ has given mankind greater privileges and joys than the devil had taken from us; this same thought is met in formula 184 (cf. 182):

> Vere dignum: in hac die, qua Iesus Christus filius tuus dominus noster divini consummato fine mysterii dispositionis antique munus explevit, ut scilicet et diabolum caelestis operis inimicum per hominem quem subiugarat elideret, et humanam reduceret ad superna [dona] substantiae: per.

The formula 202 for the feast of Pentecost also provides the basis for the proper preface for this feast in the Missale Romanum, though the ending is different in both cases. That which is common to both reads:

> Vere dignum: qui ascendit super omnes caelos sedensque ad dexteram tuam promissum Spm sanctum in filios adoptionis effudit . . .

The barriers of language and nationality are completely shattered by the work of the Spirit. The Lucan account of the events of the first Pentecost shows that he regards 'speaking with tongues' as an unmistakable sign of the gift of the Spirit.[1] The formula 217 is at one with the evangelist in seeing this event as a symbol of the renewal of that moment when speech was confounded as a result of human sin. Thus Pentecost is presented as the reverse of Babel. Gen. 11: 1–9, recalled in the words of our formula, recounts how through pride mankind lost their ability to speak one with another. The refusal to be bound together in obedience to the will of God resulted in their loss of a common language. It is Luke's contention that God wills to re-create mankind in one family and, as our formula points out, united through the power of the Holy Spirit.

The Prayer

> Benedic, domine, et has tuas creaturas . . .   (205)

is of considerable interest, coming as it does on the feast of Pentecost, for those that come up to the font. The Apostolic

[1] Acts 2: 4, cf. 10: 46, 19: 6.

Tradition of Hippolytus employs a form of benediction over the milk and honey for distribution to the newly baptized which includes similar lines of thought at one point.[1] The newly baptized are seen to have passed into the Promised Land and become heirs of the promise made to Abraham, 'I will give you a land flowing with milk and honey'. The Apostolic Tradition is certainly representative of the Roman Liturgy at an early date, as we have already witnessed; the thought of the two parallel prayers coincides at this reference to Abraham and the promise which was made to him. In the Apostolic Tradition the prayer occurs in the Paschal liturgy, whilst in the Leonianum it forms part of the liturgy of Pentecost, the other great festival upon which baptisms were performed from the second century onwards. There is no mention of this ceremony of giving a cup of milk and honey[2] to the newly baptized nor is this prayer or any trace of it to be found in the Gelasian (Vat. Reg. 316) or Gregorian Sacramentaries. The tenth-century Pontifical of Egbert of York (Paris, B.N. lat. 10575) contains this prayer almost exactly as it appears in the Leonianum; it is also to be found in an eleventh-century Pontifical from Setz (B.N. lat. 820). Both these books present evidence of the persistence of such a primitive custom until quite a late date. Some see a Biblical foundation to such a custom in the two New Testament references, 1 Pet. 2: 2, 1 Cor. 3: 2, both of which occur in a general context of instruction to those who have newly come to a knowledge of the Christian faith. In the Leonianum this particular formula of blessing is placed after the special 'communicantes' for the feast of Pentecost—there appears to be no post-communion prayer. Presumably, as in the Apostolic Tradition, the prayer is said after the Eucharist Prayer and before distribution of Holy Communion, so that at the distribution of Holy Communion the milk and honey can also be given to those who are newly baptized.

[1] Dix, op. cit., p. 40.
[2] Note that the prayer here is not unlike that of the commixture of the chalice at the Offertory: 'Deus qui humanae substantiae . .' The cup is clearly one in which the milk and honey is mixed together, thus signifying the union of heavenly and earthly 'substantia' in Jesus Christ.

IV

Group XXXIII is entitled SUPER DEFUNCTOS and contains five sets of formulae which are for use as Requiem Masses. Set i provides a Common Mass of the dead which may have been used either for the clergy or for the laity. The formula 1140 begins

> Hanc igitur oblationem illius famuli tui, quam tibi offeret pro animam famuli tui illius, quaesumus, domine, propitiatus accipias, et miserationum tuarum . . .

It seems that this prayer (which prays that the soul may enter into life ('transitum . . . ad vitam'), having been absolved from the chains of death) is meant to be inserted into the Canon of the Mass at the place where the 'hanc igitur' prayer would normally appear. But there are several places in the prayer, especially if we accept Muratori's emendation of 'offert' to 'offerunt', which are very reminiscent of the 'Memento Domine' prayer as it now appears in the Canon of the Missale Romanum. The second set is concerned with a person dying in a state of penitence. An insertion of the words 'h ig' in the margin before the formula 1143 indicates its use as an 'hanc igitur' prayer proper to the occasion. The secret prayer at the offertory prays that through the offering of the sacrifice the soul may find that pardon from all its sins which it desired so earnestly. The first three formulae of set iii (1144–6) appear to be either variants of or supplements to set ii, whilst the last four (1147–50) are supplementary to set i. The formula 1150,

> Fidelium, deus, animarum conditor et redemptor . . .

is almost identical to that used in the Missale Romanum as a general collect on All Souls' Day. The fourth set is a Requiem for a bishop, so too is that of set v. Both these may well have been used at the burial of a pope. Certainly the formula 1158,

> Hanc igitur: ut qui beati Petri apostoli sedem vicario secutus officio, tuae quoque . . .

indicates the occupant of the chair of Peter as the person to whom reference is made. For Western Christendom the Requiem Mass became a regular part of the rites of burial. No doubt the original idea pervading such prayers was the quite natural wish of those remaining in this world to continue in some way their intercourse with those now departed. It was natural that the Lord's own Eucharistic memorial should be used as the rite within which such sentiments came to be expressed. This particular concept appears strongly in the sets of formulae for the month of April, with which the Sacramentary opens. It seems likely that these formulae should be assigned to a category which may be termed 'Common of Martyrs', since on the identity of these martyrs the texts do not say anything explicit. It is clearly discernible, however, that the faithful who are present to celebrate the feast have close connections with those names they now honour. The formulae often speak of 'patrocinium' 8, 31, 63, 74, etc., 'patroni' 148, 'praesidia' 7, 39, 125, etc. The impression gained is that the celebrant has known personally, and so has his congregation, those whom he now addresses among the company of the martyrs and confessors in heavenly bliss. They are called upon to assist with their prayers those who are left in the warfare of this world:

Vere dignum: qui non solum martyrum, sed etiam confessorum tuorum es virtute mirabilis. Licet enim illi passione sint clari, qui manifestis acerva supplicia sustinuere tormentis, etiam isti tamen occultae proposito castigationis adflicti et cruciati spiritalis observantiae disciplinis illorum sunt vestigia subsecuti: per. (20.)

Vere dignum: maiestatem tuam suppliciter exorantes, ne perire patiaris, quibus tanta remedia providisti; et conlata praesidia non ad cumulum reis damnationis eveniant, sed potius ad effectum salvationis accedant: per. (39.)

For those confessors who have suffered torture in the flesh for their Christian faith the celebrant pleads that they may not have to endure the sufferings and pains hereafter:

Exaudi nos, domine deus noster . . . ut quorum celebramus triumphos, possimus retinere constantiam: per. (63.)

As a general observation it is true to say that the earliest prayers offered for the departed conceive of no obstacle which separates them in this eucharistic context from those still living. It is legitimate to commend their souls (unless they are martyrs, in which case they are already thought to enjoy the heavenly bliss) to the mercy of God. Thus prayers for repose, light, refreshment, also for forgiveness and sanctification, find their place in the early liturgies of the West and also of the East. It would be true to add that, in respect of the departed, the formal liturgical prayers of the West are more sombre and restrained than those of the East and the former are especially marked by the thought of sin and its punishment. In this the Western thought and tradition is concordant with that of the Mozarabic Missal and the Liber Ordinum, the non-Roman elements of the Gelasian Sacramentary, and the Bobbio Missal. The language of these formulae in the Leonianum makes it clear that the Eucharist is seen as a propitiatory act on behalf of those departed. At the same time the Christian hope of rest, light, peace, pardon, and deliverance from sins finds its place. The Constitution 'De Sacra Liturgia' of the Vatican Council II[1] directs that the 'rite for the burial of the dead should express more clearly the paschal character of Christian death . . .', but it is evident that by about the year A.D. 600 the liturgical prayer of the church had already almost completely lost this emphasis.

V

The contents of the formulae in group XV IN N APOSTOLORUM PETRI ET PAULI reflect the position which the see of Rome held in relation to the remainder of the Church. Both Peter and Paul are named together as the apostles upon whom the see has been founded. The traditional text of Matt. 16: 17, 18 appears in a number of the formulae and is applied in a general way to the whole Church, which is founded upon the solid foundation of the apostles (chiefly in this context Peter and Paul):

Omnipotens sempiterne deus, qui aeclesiam tuam in apostolica soliditate fundatam ab infernarum erues terrore portarum . . . (332.)

Passages taken from scripture which relate to the lives of both Peter and Paul are quoted in the proper prefaces and especially in 285 and 294. The chief event in the life of St. Peter which is called to mind is his confession at Caesarea Philippi and the Lord's commission consequent upon that confession; for St. Paul, formula 294 recalls the account of Acts 9: 1–8 and the

---

[1] Cf. *Ephem. Lit.* 78 (1964), p. 208: iii. 81 (Ordo exsequiarum) 'Ritus exsequiarum paschalem mortis christianae indolem manifestius exprimat . . .'

sudden conversion of Paul on the Damascus road; 'vas electionis'[1] is the title given to Paul (374). However, in spite of their distinctive lives, the injunctions of James 2: 5 and 1 Cor. 1: 26 provide a reminder that God chose

non mundi reges et proceres, non facundos aut divites, sed abiectos et pauperes, ineruditos adque ignobiles . . . (294.)

Throughout this group the assertion is constantly made that the Church is built upon the solid foundation of the apostles and this apostolic foundation is seen as the assurance that a Church thus grounded may fear nothing from false and erroneous doctrine:

Vere dignum: tu enim tribues, domine, ut praedicationis apostolicae claritatem nulla iuris inferni subdola doctrina commaculet, nulla praevaricatio veritatis offuscet: per. (300.)

The feast being celebrated is that of SS. Peter and Paul: the Roman church is celebrating the feast with great joy, since these are the founders of their own community that they honour:

Omnipotens sempiterne deus, qui ineffabili sacramento ius apostolici principatus in Romani nominis arce posuisti, unde se evangelica veritas per tota mundi . . . (292.)

The references in this formula to the position of the see of Rome in relation to the whole Church can be matched elsewhere (cf. 307, 282, 343, 319). The formula 348 is especially telling:

Vere dignum: qui, ut hanc sedem regimen aeclesiae totius efficeris, et quod haec praedicasset ostenderis ubique servandum, simul in ea et apostolicae principem dignitatis et magistrum gentium collocasti: per.

Batiffol[2] says of the formula 348 that 'il donne toute sa plénitude de sens au "principatus" du Siège apostolique', and quotes a further passage from this group to support this statement:

Vere dignum . . . ut beatorum apostolorum Petri et Pauli gloriosa confessio, cuius annua vota celebramus, nec capiatur umquam falsis nec perturbetur adversis; sed ut potius tui corporis ubique devota conpago te dispensante suscipiat, quod sedis illa censuerit, quam tenere voluisti totius aeclesiae principatum: per. (343.)

[1] Acts 9: 15.   [2] Batiffol, *Cathedra Petri* (Paris, 1938), p. 92.

The similarity in thought between these formulae and certain of the African writers is very striking. Both Cyprian and Optatus speak of the See of Rome as 'cathedra principalis' or 'ecclesia principalis'. For Cyprian the 'cathedra Petri' is both the 'ecclesia principalis' and the place 'unde unitas sacerdotalis exorta est'.[1] The collegiate nature of episcopacy is an important concept for such writers, and the Petrine office, as manifested by the see of Rome, is seen in this light. The position of the bishop within his local community and diocese is viewed in much the same terms as that of Peter within the apostolic band and now of the successor of Peter, the bishop of Rome, in relation to the rest of his fellow bishops. Batiffol[2] makes the point that in the writings of Cyprian and Optatus the term 'principalis' is to be understood in temporal terms, as he considers Tertullian and Irenaeus had done before them. Certainly such a formula as 280 ('Deus, qui hunc diem . . .') would support this view. It is perhaps worth pointing out at this stage the dialogue at present in progress concerning this precise point. Küng[3] mentions the two principles of unity in the church, the one which is the bond between the bishops, with their local churches, and the Petrine office; and the other the bond between the bishops and their local churches with each other. It is this perspective, together with a more critical appraisal of the Petrine office within the apostolic band, as it is recounted in the New Testament, which is being closely examined in the current oecumenical debate, in order to arrive at a clearer understanding not only of the Petrine office but also of the episcopal office and its relation to the whole Christian community.

[1] Cyprian, *Ep*. lix. 14.
[2] Batiffol, op. cit., p. 113: 'Elle est "principalis" parce que la "cathedra" que Pierre y a installée est la "cathedra" la première en date, celle que le Christ a établie et donnée à Pierre: la "cathedra" type et norme de toutes les autres; "cathedra principalis" ou "ecclesia principalis", c'est tout un.'
[3] H. Küng, *The Living Church* (London, 1953), pp. 333–69.

9

THE PROBLEM OF AUTHORSHIP
AND DATE

THE problem concerning the authorship and date of the Leonine Sacramentary may be considered in two different ways. There is in the first instance the question as to who composed the various groups of Mass formulae in the Sacramentary. Here there are a number of indications of authorship and date, though scholars are not always unanimous in their verdict upon any particular group. An outline of some of the main contributions in this field is given below; other particular problems of authorship and date have already been examined in detail at an earlier stage. It is clear that many of these groups once existed as independent units and that these have later been brought together by the compiler of the Sacramentary. This leads us to the second question which must be posed, namely the identity of the compiler of the Sacramentary and the date of its compilation. Suggestions concerning the compiler of the Sacramentary as a whole have been few, yet at the same time diverse. Buchwald, as we have already seen, suggested Gregory of Tours,[1] whilst Rule suggested that the complete work as it now exists is the result of recensions of the work of Leo, Hilary, and Simplicius.[2] But in the absence of any positive evidence within the manuscript itself in support of these views, they can at best be only very tentative.

From our previous discussion it will be clear that evidence relating to the authorship and date of individual groups of Mass formulae in the Sacramentary is not entirely lacking. Indeed the name 'Leonine' first became attached to the Sacramentary by its first editor, Bianchini, who recognized at once the obvious

---

[1] R. Buchwald, 'Das Sacramentarium Leonianum und sein Verhältnis zu den beiden andern römischen Sakramentarien', *Weidenauer Studien*, 2 (1908), pp. 185–251.

[2] M. Rule in *J.T.S.* 9 (1908), pp. 515–56; 10 (1909), pp. 54–99.

parallels between parts of the text and some of the writings of Pope Leo. These are chiefly to be found within the groups X (ORATIONES PRIDIE PENTECOSTEN) and XII (IN IEIUNIO MENSIS QUARTI). The formula 207 of group XII reads:

Concede nobis, domine, praesidia militiae christianae sanctis incoare ieiuniis, ut contra spiritales nequitias pugnatori continentiae muniamur auxiliis: per. ;

and in *Sermon* lxxviii. 2. the following passage occurs:

. . . hi itaque doctores qui exemplis et traditionibus suis omnes ecclesiae filios imbuerunt tirocinium militiae christianae sanctis inchoarere ieiuniis ut contra spiritales nequitias pugnaturi abstinentiae annua caperent.

A second example of this form of parallelism is afforded by the formula 226,

Adesto, domine, supplicibus tuis, ut hoc sollemne ieiunium, quod animis corporibusque curandis salubriter institutum est, devoto servitio celebremus: per.,

and *Sermo* lxxviii. 1. 3,

. . . sollemne ieiunium quod animis corporibusque curandis salubriter institutum devota nobis est observantia celebrandum . . .

However, perhaps the most extensive of these parallels appears in the formula 229,

Vere dignum: post illos enim laetitiae dies, quos in honorem domini a mortuis resurgentis et in coelos ascendentis exigimus, postque perceptum sancti spiritus donum necessariae nobis haec ieiunia sancta provisa sunt, ut pura conversatione viventibus quae divinitus aeclesiae sunt collata permaneant: per.,

and *Sermo* lxxviii. 3:

. . . post sanctae laetitiae dies quos in honorem Domini a mortuis resurgentis ac deinde in caelos ascendentis exegimus postque perceptum sancti spiritus donum salubriter et necessarie consuetudo est ordinata ieiunii . . . ut illa in nobis quae hac die ecclesiae divinitus sunt collata permaneant.

The Ballerini have been led to suggest the Leonine authorship of the formula 361 because of the similarity in thought and expression to the rebuke found in Leo's sermon[1] preached on the octave day of the feast of SS. Peter and Paul. In the sermon Leo makes reference to the Vandal attack upon Rome in A.D. 455 under Genseric, and the deliverance in which he played so important a part. He rebukes the people for their being so ungrateful as to neglect the feast-day of the apostles, even though it was the anniversary of their deliverance from that time of terror and distress.

A study of the formula 'Deus, castorum corporum benignus habitator . . .' (1104) within the section XXX entitled AD VIRGINES SACRAS has been made by O. G. Harrison.[2] Callewaert,[3] de Puniet,[4] and Coebergh[5] all consider that this preface is the work of Pope Leo (c. A.D. 460); they do so on grounds of vocabulary and style. The formula 1104 is undoubtedly very similar in this respect to the Nativity sermons. The words 'humanam substantiam' occur very frequently in the writings of Pope Leo; so too do such words as 'condicione', 'sumpserunt', 'licentia', 'sublimiores', 'generis', etc. Again the use of the word 'sacramentum' to signify 'a holy thing' such as the mystery of the Incarnation (the 'sublimiores animae' who 'concupiscerent sacramentum') is typical of Leo's style. 'Auctor' as a divine title is also frequently used in the sermons. We can say with certainty that Leo's vocabulary is to be found in the formula 'Deus, castorum corporum . . .', as also is his dignified style and cursus.[6] However, it seems to Harrison that Leo's work is preserved in the Gelasian (Vat. Reg. 316) rather than in the Leonine Sacramentary. Both Vat. Reg. 316 and the Leonianum are parallel as far as the words 'hanc flammam', where Vat. Reg. 316 gives the reading 'per liberum arbitrium hunc amorem virginitatis', which Harrison maintains is more true to Pope Leo, since 'arbitrium' is one of his words, while 'flammam' in place of 'amorem' is not. In this respect it is interesting to note

---

[1] Leo, *Sermo* lxxxiv (Migne *P.L.* 54. 433), 'In octavis apostolorum Petri et Pauli; De neglecta solemnitate'.

[2] O. G. Harrison, 'The formulas "Ad Virgines Sacras". A Study of the sources', *Ephem. Lit.* 66 (1952), pp. 252–73.

[3] C. Callewaert, 'S. Léon le Grand et les textes du Léonien', *Sacris Erudiri*, 1 (1948), pp. 36–164.

[4] P. de Puniet, *Le Pontifical Romain*, vol. 2 (Louvain–Paris, 1931), pp. 162–71.

[5] C. Coebergh, 'Saint Léon le Grand auteur de la grande formule "Ad Virgines Sacras" du sacramentaire léonien', *Sacris Erudiri*, 6 (1954), pp. 282–326.

[6] See Appendix B, pp. 154–7.

that the use of the word 'flammam' in the Leonianum is repeated again in the same context in the Pontifical of Egbert of
York (Paris, B.N. lat. 10575), though the text of Vat. Reg. 316
has 'amorem', as do the others. It is suggested that the use of
this word in this particular context indicates an early Roman
origin at least for part of the formula, since it recalls the bridal
'flammam' with which a fourth-country Roman would be quite
familiar. However, Harrison states that there is good reason
for considering Pope Leo to be the author of the formula
'Deus, castorum . . .' in the form in which it has come down
to us. It is likely, though, that he incorporated older material,
and this is the nucleus from which the present prayer has
been formed. He maintains that the paragraph 'sit in eis
. . . eligere super omnia: per.' is quite different from the rest of
the text and that these short, well-balanced phrases were intended to be sung—they fit perfectly the traditional melody of
the 'cantus ferialis'. Essentially, however, this extract has its
origins with the North African bishop of Carthage, Cyprian, in
the mid third century. Though there are no exact parallel
phrases with his treatise 'De Habitu Virginum', the thought
expressed in both is very similar. In all probability this paragraph was a form of blessing, used in the fourth and fifth centuries, and finally incorporated into this prayer by Pope Leo,
whose dignified style seems obvious in the present version of the
formula, at least as far as the passage 'sit in eis'.

Passing reference has already been made to the contribution
of Coebergh[1] to the question of authorship. Many of the formulae he attributes to the work of Gelasius (A.D. 492–6). Evidence
for such a hypothesis he finds in the formulae of group XXVIII
(Ordination prayers), which he considers belong to the 'sacramentorum praefationes et orationes'; the *Liber Pontificalis*
attributes these to Gelasius. Coebergh asserts Gelasius as the
author of almost all the sets of Mass formulae in section XVIII
for the month of July, as well as those of sections XXVII and
XLIII for the Ember days of September and December. Most
of the foregoing conclusions are based upon comparisons of

---

[1] C. Coebergh, 'S. Gélase premier auteur du soi-disant sacramentaire léonien',
Ephem. Lit. 64 (1950), pp. 214–37. Cf. also 'S. Gélase premier auteur de plusieures
messes et prières du sacramentaire léonien', *Ephem. Lit.* 65 (1951), pp. 171–81; 'Le
pape saint Gélase premier auteur de plusieures messes et préfaces du soi-disant
sacramentaire léonien', *Sacris Erudiri*, 4 (1952), pp. 46–102.

style and vocabulary. Before Coebergh, however, Capelle[1] had already studied the formulae 75–8 and 515–20 and had come to the conclusion that they were Gelasian. He asserts that the formulae of both sets are strictly unified, having a common spirit which pervades them all—indeed a title which would be conveniently applicable to formulae 75–8 might be 'Missa pro errantibus'. All the prayers are directed against the Christian capitulation to pagan influences and the dangers attendant upon such faithful Christians in performing acts incompatible with their baptismal promises. There are many expressions characteristic of Gelasius which distinguish themselves from the usual vocabulary of the formulae in the sacramentary such as 'respuere' (3 times), 'profanitas' (twice), 'retinere' (3 times), 'depravare' (once), and 'pronuntiare' (once), all of which occur in the formulae 75, 76, 515, 516, and are used by Pope Leo very sparingly (as indicated in the brackets) whilst Gelasius uses them constantly. A second point which Capelle presents in favour of the Gelasian authorship of the set of formulae 75–8 concerns the phrase 'cunctis qui christiana professione censentur'. He notes the use of the word 'censeri' directly with the ablative, in the sense of 'to be judged of such quality', as being a regular feature of the Gelasian style. Leo, however, does not follow this construction; he always adds 'in' before the ablative or 'inter' before the accusative.[2] Again, Capelle asserts that Gelasius always uses the word 'permixtus' (77) to imply heretics and pagans whilst Leo never uses it in this context. The particular form of the restrictive proposition, 'sic . . . permixta agitur, ut tamen . . . cavenda' (77), is a further device used regularly by Gelasius but never by Leo. The formula 76 is an excellent piece of coherent literary work, using 'mensa, convivium, gustus, epulae', clearly inspired by the eucharistic mystery of which it formed a part. The phrase 'mensa participere' of that same formula is reminiscent of the phrase in 1 Cor. 10: 21, 'non

---

[1] B. Capelle, 'Messes du pape S. Gélase dans le sacramentaire léonien', *Rev bénédictine*, 56 (1945–6), pp. 12–41.

[2] The five rare cases when Leo does use the word 'censeo' are quoted here:

    (*a*) 'nec in sacrarum numero censeantur'
    (*b*) 'nec inter catholicos censeatur'
    (*c*) 'nec potest in filiorum dei adoptione censeri'
    (*d*) 'sed in diaboli parte censetur'
    (*e*) 'censetur qualitas actionis'

potestis mensae Domini participes esse, et mensae daemoniorum'. Capelle points out that on four occasions when Gelasius protests against any compromise with heresy or paganism he has this same antithesis in mind, viz. 'mensa Domini . . . mensa daemoniorum'. Leo, often writing along the same lines, never uses the quotation in such a context; indeed when the occasion presents itself he uses 'nulla unquam . . . iniquitati cum aequalitate communio . . . nullus est tenebris cum luce consensus', which is more consonant with another Pauline quotation (2 Cor. 6: 14).

The general sense of the second set of Mass prayers (515–20) is similar to that which has just been discussed. The sincerity of professing the Christian name is threatened by the pagan 'profanitates', by the 'falsa gaudia', and by this 'simulatio diabolica'. Capelle considers that the unity of the set is once again without question. The situation created in Rome by the continuing of the Lupercalia festival and the offensive launched against the survival of this pagan custom by Gelasius himself is paralleled by the situation envisaged by the author of these particular formulae. The 'pravitas' of formulae 516 is not to be understood in the sense of moral waywardness and depravity, but rather as indicative of false and erroneous doctrine with which the church was threatened. In a similar way the word 'pravitas' occurs again in the formula 625. Indeed the proper preface (623) is again suggestive of the festival of Lupercalia:

. . . dum scilicet vel aguntur crimina vel canuntur. Promtiusque debemus, omni ritu pestifere vetustatis abolito, caelestis vitae novitate gaudere . . .

Throughout the formulae 620–5 there is clear evidence of the style of Gelasius (that is if we are prepared to accept the criteria of Capelle—usage of particular words, sentence structure, etc.). A further literary device used by Gelasius is illustrated by the following examples: 'veris' and 'falsisque' separated by 'confessoribus'; 'pollutam' and 'permixtamque' separated by 'simul'. Examples of this type appear frequently in the writings of Gelasius.

In this way Capelle illustrates three sets of Mass formulae which by their distinctive style can be attributed to Gelasius:

75–8, 515–20, and 620–5. Antoine Chavasse,[1] however, ascribes a further sixteen sets of Mass formulae in the groups XXIX and XVIII to the hand of Gelasius; the criteria of this selection are the features of style and historical allusions contained within the formulae. Examples of such sets to be found in section XXIX are ix, xiii, xv, xix, etc. Aided by a study of the historical references within the text, Chavasse ascribes many of the formulae to Pope Vigilius (A.D. 537–55). At least sixty sets of Mass formulae were probably composed during the years A.D. 537–8. There are a further nine sets which, it is considered, commemorate anniversaries of the consecration of the pope, celebrated between the years A.D. 538 and 545. These have been given a fuller treatment in another section, since the Mass formulae also provide important evidence regarding the date of that part of the Sacramentary.[2] In this section XXIX Chavasse considers there are nine sets of prayers, in addition to those relating to the anniversary of an episcopal ordination, which can be attributed to Vigilius: x, xi, xii, xiv, xvi, xvii, xviii, xxi, and xxiii. These sets follow immediately the section 'In natale episcoporum' and it is considered that their position here is indicative of a similarity in style and ideas; they particularly resemble the anniversary Mass iv, and hence Chavasse places them in the same year, A.D. 538. This Mass (iv) was composed after the siege of Rome on the 4 March A.D. 538 for the anniversary on the 29 March following; similarly these nine Mass sets, he thinks, have been composed after the deliverance of Rome. There are numerous phrases within the individual formulae which indicate this possibility:

qui nos ab hostibus defendes inmeritos   (1021)

et cunctis hostibus caelesti virtute conpressis aumentum nobis tribue religionis et pacis   (1033)

pro concessis beneficiis exhibentes gratias, et pro concendendis suppliciter depraecantes   (1098)

In fact these nine sets of formulae are sufficient in number for the Sundays which follow Easter (celebrated in A.D. 538 on 4 April) to Sunday, 27 June of that same year. The following

---

[1] See above, p. 63.
[2] See above, pp. 78 ff.

chart taken from Chavasse, will serve as an example of his classification of these formulae as regards authorship and date:

			(sets of formulae)
29 March 538		(Group) XXIX	iiii (Consec. of Vigilius)
4 April	Easter		
11 April	Low Sunday (Easter I)	XVIII	xxvii
18 April	Easter II	XXIX	x
25 April	Easter III		xi
2 May	Easter IV		xii
9 May	Easter V		xiv
16 May	Easter VI		xvi
23 May	Pentecost		—
30 May	Pentecost I		—
6 June	Pentecost II		xvii
13 June	Pentecost III		xviii
20 June	Pentecost IV		xxi
27 June	Pentecost V		xxiii
29 June	SS. Peter and Paul		Ad virgines sacras

The six sets of formulae entitled DE SICCITATE TEMPORIS (XXXII,)
which appear at the opening of October, are all to be ascribed
to the hand of Vigilius. Clearly, it is only the first of these sets
which is consonant with the title of this section. It is known that
in the year A.D. 538 there was an exceptional drought and at the
same time famine afflicted much of the region round Rome.

Chavasse argues that the compilation of the book as a whole
could not have been made earlier than Vigilius (d. A.D. 545) or
later than John III (A.D. 561–74), since there is no provision of
formulae for the feast-day of SS. Philip and James, and John III
had dedicated a basilica in their honour, thus inaugurating their
cultus. He considers that the Mass prayers attributed to Gelasius were probably incorporated into the collection during the
pontificate of Pelagius I (A.D. 556–61). Dom Antonio Coelho[1]
supports the view that a large number of the Masses within the
Sacramentary were composed during the time of the invasion
of the Ostrogoths. He then goes on to mention the burial or
anniversary of the burial of Pope Simplicius (A.D. 468–83) as the
occasion commemorated by one of the formulae (1163). But as

---

[1] A. Coelho, *Cours de Liturgie Romaine*, vol. i (Saint-André–Paris, 1928), XXI, p. 252.

Feltoe suggests, since this is one formula among three with the general title XXXIV SCI SILVESTRI it is more probably another case of defective adaptation.

Bourque,[1] in his study of the Leonianum, contributes much valuable information regarding the context within which the sets of formulae have arisen and the date of their composition. Much of the material in the Sacramentary is Roman in origin and therefore the question arises as to whether it is a product of the city churches in Rome, the suburban areas where the catacombs are located, or the papal liturgy itself. In fact, not all the formulae can be ascribed to one of these exclusively as its place of origin but all three have contributed to the material now collected together in the Sacramentary. Thus for example the formulae of the feast of SS. Peter and Paul are considered to be papal in their origin, as the following extract indicates:

> Vere dignum: qui, ut hanc sedem regimen aeclesiae totius efficeris, et quod haec praedicasset ostenderis ubique servandum, simul in ea et apostolicae principem dignitatis et magistrum gentium collocasti: per.   (348.)

Since there are allusions from time to time in this group to the invasions of the barbarians against the city of Rome during the first part of the fifth century, Bourque concludes that the formulae contained therein are to be dated just after the mid fifth century. At least this date will serve as an *ante quem non*; in respect of his dating, Bourque is never at any stage any more precise than this. There are eight sets of formulae which appear in connection with the feast-day of St. Sixtus and his companions. These will serve as an example of those formulae which Bourque considers have definite connections with the catacombs, in this particular case the catacombs of Callistus and Praetextatus on the Via Appia, as the title to the group (XX) illustrates and also the preface of the first formula:

> Vere dignum: quoniam inter innumeras toto mundo martyrum palmas, quibus orbis huius praecipue coronatus est ambitus . . . (706.)

In view of the references within the formulae of this group (cf. 716, 725, 730, 732, 736) to a state of affairs which reflects troubled times, Bourque ventures to suggest that the date which

---

[1] Bourque, op. cit., pp. 64–169.

can most reasonably be assigned to these prayers is that of the siege of Ricimer in July A.D. 472.

Finally, as an example of a group of formulae which had its origin within the city of Rome, the cultus of St. Cecilia may be considered. Undoubtedly the origins of the cultus of this saint are very difficult to determine exactly. But it is likely that the cultus centred around the burial-place of a certain Cecilia, foundress of the 'titulus Caeciliae'. Bourque suggests that the date of the formulae must be after the appearance of her 'acta', upon which the formula 1172 looks as if it is based.[1] Thus a date of the end of the fifth century is perhaps the most likely.

The above are three examples of the way in which Bourque orders his material in putting forward his theory concerning the origins of the individual parts of the Sacramentary. He fixes a *terminus post quem* for each of the groups and at the same time indicates whether their origin is from the papal liturgy, the liturgy of the cemeteries, or the liturgy of one of the city churches. The earliest groups are those compiled for the feasts of the Ascension, the Quattro Coronati, and S. Clement, all of which are to be dated about the year A.D. 400. The last of the sections to be compiled was the 'libellus' for September (to be dated about the year A.D. 560) which is of papal origin. Having provided extracts from the text concerning its papal composition, Bourque goes on to give this section the date of A.D. 560 from the evidence provided by the sets of Mass formulae entitled 'In natale episcoporum'. These are to be ascribed to the hand of Pelagius I (A.D. 556–61), who was consecrated on Easter Day (16 April A.D. 556). As we have already seen, Chavasse attributes this particular group to Pope Vigilius; however, there is a fuller discussion of this set of formulae elsewhere.[2] In respect of the date of the material, even if it is Vigilian, it is still within the middle of the sixth century.

If we are thinking of the author merely in terms of the volume of material provided by any particular hand, then both Vigilius and Gelasius have a better claim to the authorship of the Sacramentary than Leo, who had traditionally been associated with its composition. Certainly we cannot subscribe to the statement that Leo is the author of the Sacramentary. On the other hand parallels with his work have been noted and where these paral-

---

[1] See above, p. 50 n. 3.   [2] See above, pp. 78 ff.

lels do occur the possibility is strong that the liturgical text appeared first and during the course of the sermon the collect for the day was quoted.[1] We are familiar with this technique in our own day. In some cases the text of the collect may be quoted direct, in others we find that some words have been changed or perhaps even omitted altogether. There is certainly much to be said in favour of Bourque's treatment of the material in the Sacramentary, particularly where the titles indicate some link with a building or area which is clearly related to the city of Rome. The contents of those particular formulae seem to support such a point of view. However, this theory would presuppose that much of the material is Roman in its origin, but a discussion of this point must be held over until a later chapter.[2] Nevertheless we can say with certainty that the authorship of the formulae within the Leonianum cannot be supposed to have been the work of one person: it is no more the work of Gelasius or Vigilius than it is the work of Leo. Clearly it is a composite work and a number of hands are evident within the whole book. The date of the material embodied within the Leonianum ranges from the mid third century (Cyprian of Carthage) to the late sixth century (Gregory I, c. A.D. 590).

Though Probst and Buchwald were particularly inclined to attribute a large number of the formulae to Damasus (A.D. 366–84), a detailed study of the question of authorship and date indicates that without doubt Leo, Gelasius, and Vigilius were the chief contributors of material. The names of other popes must also be included, Zosimus (417–18), Boniface I (418–22), Sixtus III (432–40), Hilary (461–8), Simplicius (468–83), Felix III (483–92), and Symmachus (498–514); and, though in each case their contributions are by no means numerous, they may have been the authors of some of the formulae. One important point which does emerge from a study of possible authors of parts of the Sacramentary is that the number of non-Roman, one might almost say non-papal, contributions is almost negligible. Obviously this is a fact which must be considered in any discussion of the place of origin of the text of the Sacramentary.

The second question concerning the compilation of the Sacramentary as a whole is surrounded by innumerable difficulties,

---

[1] Cf. F. L. Cross, 'The Pre-Leonine Elements in the Proper of the Roman Mass', *J.T.S.* 50 (1949), pp. 191–7.   [2] See below, pp. 133 ff.

not the least being the lack of evidence, either internal or external, which could perhaps have provided some basis for investigation. No doubt the view expressed by Probst is correct, namely that the compiler was not a cleric. It is difficult to see why, if the compiler was a cleric, as Dix supposes,[1] there are so many examples of misplaced material. Again the erratic way in which the compiler actually sets out his material in the book has been noted earlier. There is no one method of arrangement of the material: various methods obtain—by month, by the enumeration of different items, and by the liturgical year (this is done very roughly and in thef ramework of the civil year). The text has clearly been worked over a second time, most likely by the compiler himself, and various adjustments have been made at this stage.[2] A clear example of such a point is the short title 'Preces in S. Eufymiae' in group XXIV (SS. Cornelius and Cyprian) which indicates that the formula following is misplaced and belongs to the next group (XXV). Whether the compilation of the Sacramentary was done by one of the authors of a particular group of Mass formulae it is impossible to say. The marginal notes of the manuscript only provide the very sparse information that the manuscript had definite connections with Verona during the eighth century and the book was at some time connected with Egino, its bishop. Concerning the date of the compilation itself, we must ultimately rely on the palaeographical evidence. Both Lowe[3] and Bischoff[4] are agreed that the manuscript is to be dated about the year A.D. 600. If Bourque is correct in dating the last collection of material about the year 560 (and there certainly seems to be support for the view that material was contributed by Vigilius about the middle of the sixth century, and this is independent of Bourque's conclusions), then very little time has lapsed between this last composition of material (independent of the whole collection) and the compilation of the Sacramentary as a whole. From the present discussion, the most likely date for the compilation of the Sacramentary seems the end of the sixth century; apart from this no more definite date can be given.

---

[1] G. Dix, O.S.B., *The Shape of the Liturgy* (London, 1945), pp. 567–8.
[2] See above, pp. 3–4.
[3] E. A. Lowe, op. cit. iv (Oxford, 1947), p. 32 n. 514.
[4] B. Bischoff in K. Gamber, 'Sakramentartypen', *Texte und Arbeiten*, 49/50, p. 48.

10

LITERARY PARALLELS IN
THE LEONIANUM
AND OTHER LITURGICAL BOOKS

WITHIN the Leonine Sacramentary itself there are 469
formulae which are peculiar to that work and not found
in any other extant liturgical manuscript. But out of a
total of 1,331 formulae contained in the Leonianum, 175 recur
in the propers of the present-day Missale Romanum together
with three other prayers, 'Aufer a nobis' (985), 'Deus, qui
humanae substantiae' (1239), and 'Quod ore sumpsimus' (531),
which have passed into the Ordinary of the Mass. The 175
which occur in the Missale Romanum are included in the 862
formulae which other liturgical books have in common with
the Leonianum. Doublets or near doublets of formulae in other
books with the Leonine Sacramentary are to be found chiefly
in manuscripts such as Vat. Reg. 316, Paris, B.N. lat. 816
(Angoulême), Prague O 83, St. Gall 348, and Paris, B.N. lat.
12048 (Gellone) so far as the 'Gelasian' type are concerned, and
in Cambrai 164, Vat. Ottobonianus 313, and Vat. Reg. 337 of
the 'Gregorian' type. These may be conveniently grouped under
the general heading of 'Roman' sources. Less frequently, however, formulae to be found in the Leonianum appear also in
what might be termed 'non-Roman' sources. Examples of these
books are as follows: Codex Bergamensis, Codex A 24 of the
Ambrosiana (Milan) as representative of the 'Ambrosian' type;
Vat. Reg. 317 (Missale Gothicum), Vat. Reg. 257 (Missale
Francorum), and Cod. Vat. Palatinus 493 (Missale Gallicanum Vetus) which are Gallican in origin; and finally the
'Celtic' type as represented by the Bobbio Missal (Paris, B.N.
lat. 13246), the Missale Drummondiense, the Rosslyn Missal,
and the Stowe Missal (Cod. D II 3 Royal Irish Academy,
Dublin).

Certain of the formulae within the Leonine Sacramentary are reproduced exactly in many of the other books. One good example of such a formula is 523,

Sacrificium tibi, domine, celebrandum placatus intende; quod et nos a vitiis nostrae condicionis emundet, et tuo nomini reddat acceptos: per.

which is found, without any signs of further editing, in Vat. Reg. 316, Angoulême, Prague O 83, Gellone, St. Gall 348, Berlin (Phillipps 1667), Padua D 47, Bergomensis, Missale Gallicanum Vetus, Bobbio, and Stowe. But though this is not the only example to be found in the Leonianum of formulae which are reproduced exactly in other liturgical works, more often than not the text may be found to have been edited slightly; possibly by a mere change in word or the insertion of a further phrase into the prayer or perhaps the exclusion of a certain phrase, whilst the prayer is still, in structure at least, basically the same as that to be found in the Leonianum. There is a certain fluidity about these prayers which makes them adaptable for use either on some specific occasion or on some more general occasion A good example is the following prayer from the section entitled IN NATALE APOSTOLORUM PETRI ET PAULI (286):

Oblationes populi tui, domine, quesumus, apostolorum tuorum passio beata conciliet; et quae nostris minus [non] apta[e] sunt meritis, fiant tibi placitae tuorum depraecatione iustorum: per.

This appears in Vat. Reg. 316[1] as the offertory prayer ('secreta') on the feast-day of SS. Peter and Paul:

Oblationes populi tui, domine, quaesumus, beatorum apostolorum Petri et Pauli passio beata conciliet: et quae nostris non apta sunt meritis fiant tibi placita tuorum deprecatione iustorum: per.

Among the non-Roman sources the prayer is to be found in the Missale Gothicum (Vat. Reg. 317)[2] as the collect 'Ad Pacem' for a Mass entitled 'Missa de Plures Confessores':

Oblaciones familiae tuae, domine, quasomus beatissimorum sanctorum tuorum confessio beata conciliet et quae nostris minus

---

[1] Mohlberg, *Sacramentarium Gelasianum*, formula 923.
[2] Mohlberg, *Missale Gothicum*, formula 470.

apta sunt meritis, fiant tibi placitae tuorum dipraecacione iustorum: per.

The prayer finally reappears in the Missale Romanum as the offertory prayer ('secreta') for the feast of St. James the Apostle:

Oblationes populi tui, quaesumus, domine, beati Jacobi Apostoli passio beata conciliet: et quae nostris non aptae sunt meritis, fiant tibi placitae eius deprecatione: per.

These four examples are clearly not independent compositions. Each must depend upon the others in some way, but it is unlikely that the prayer first occurred in the Leonianum and from this manuscript passed into the Vat. Reg. 316 and so on.[1] Indeed the Vat. Reg. 316 form of the prayer is also found in four further manuscripts, twice in Angoulême (Paris, B.N. lat. 816) and Prague O 83, twice in Gellone (Paris, B.N. lat. 12048), and once in St. Gall 348. Except for minor details the prayer is the same in each manuscript, though, as can be seen from the examples above, the occasion is not always the same. In the Leonianum the formula is in the position of the Offertory ('secreta'), just before the proper preface; in fact in the Leonianum there are two formulae only (286 and 287) in that particular set. Throughout the formula's occurrence in other liturgical books the same position is preserved—at the offertory. Though in the Leonianum the prayer appears in the group entitled IN NATALE APOSTOLORUM PETRI ET PAULI there is no specific reference in the prayer itself to those apostles. It could, presumably, have been employed on the feast-day of any apostle and martyr, as indeed is found in the Roman Missal for the feast of St. James. In the Missale Gothicum (Vat. Reg. 317), however, the occasion of the formula becomes more general, 'de plures confessores'. The position of the prayer is slightly different in the Gallican structure; it becomes a prayer 'ad Pacem' which precedes the Eucharistic prayer.

Formulae which have been composed for particular occasions and preserved in the Leonianum in their original form have also found a place in the liturgical books of a later date. The set of formulae (443–8) provides Mass prayers which are clearly set within the context of a hostile invasion, not upon any city, but

---

[1] This point, however, is discussed more fully in the chapter following, pp. 140 ff.

upon Rome itself.[1] Four of these formulae are used in later books
as prayers 'In tempore belli'.[2] Thus there is a movement of
liturgical prayer, in the first instance composed for a particular
event (as in the case of 443–8 the siege of Vitiges in A.D. 537/8
is suggested), to the more general application 'In tempore belli'.
With this movement there is the complete reversal of the prac-
tice of early liturgical prayer. The later liturgical manuscripts
often contained sets of Mass formulae with a more general title,
such as those 'In tempore belli', which are available for use
during any particular time of war.

A study of the actual prayers of ordination for bishops, priests,
and deacons contained in the Leonianum and in the other
liturgical books leads to the conclusion that by the beginning of
the seventh century there was an almost uniform rite of ordination to these three 'major' orders throughout the Western
Church. Botte[3] makes the point that the pure Roman rite is
represented by the Leonine Sacramentary and the Gregorian
Sacramentary (Vat. Reg. 337). In fact the formulae

> Deus honorum omnium . . . (947) [for the consecration of a
> bishop]

> Domine, sancte pater . . . (954) [for the ordination of a priest, and]

> Adesto, quaesumus, omnipotens deus . . . (951) [for the ordination
> of a deacon]

are all found in the Gelasian (Vat. Reg. 316)[4] and Missale
Francorum (Vat. Reg. 257),[5] but with the addition of certain
other prayers; also in the prayer for the ordination of a bishop
(947) there is an interpolation

> sint speciosi muneri tuo pedes . . . de profectu omnium conse-
> quantur

between the words 'sinceritas pacis' and 'Tribuas eis cathe-
dram' of the Leonianum. This interpolation is foreign to
the pure Roman rite and contains a number of biblical quotations which serve to highlight the function of the bishop—to

[1] See above, p. 55.
[2] In the manuscript Paris, B.N. lat. 9488, fol. 11; also in *The Gregorian Sacramentary*, ed. Wilson, p. 140.   [3] See above, p. 92, n. 3.
[4] Mohlberg, *Sacramentarium Gelasianum*, formulae 769, 145/6, 152/4.
[5] *Missale Francorum*, ed. Mohlberg (Rerum Ecclesiasticarum Documenta, Series
Maior, Fontes II, Rome, 1957), Nos. 40, 30, 23.

preach the gospel, to exercise the power of binding and loosing. There are in addition smaller points of difference, such as we have seen occur when similar collects appear in other liturgical books, e.g. a difference in vocabulary here and there and a re-arrangement of certain phrases. It is in the Gallican books[1] that these Roman prayers are preserved, but in addition the ordina-tion rite has become more complex, with the resulting profusion of prayers so typical of such books. The important point, how-ever, for the present discussion is the survival of virtually the same prayer at the several ordinations of bishop, priest, and deacon, except for the interpolation mentioned above, through-out the whole of the Latin West even to the present Roman Pontifical.

Having considered briefly some of the literary parallels be-tween the Leonine Sacramentary and other liturgical books, we must now examine some of the doublets which occur within the text of the Leonine Sacramentary itself. The parallels are usually to be found in connection with one formula, though occasionally almost a whole set is reproduced elsewhere in the text.[2] However, in order to examine some of the problems in-volved in the reduplication of formulae one of the prayers for the feast of SS. Peter and Paul is to be taken by way of illustra-tion. At the same time it must be realized that, in view of their form and content, different problems are raised by different collects.

The starting-point then is the collect 'Deus, qui hunc diem . . .' (280) which opens the first collection of Mass prayers for the feast day of SS. Peter and Paul. Parallels to this collect within the Leonianum can be found in 303 and 357, whilst the phrase 'aeclesiam tuam toto terrarum orbe diffusam' is also to be found in 989 and 993 (which are in themselves two copies of virtually the same prayer, the only difference being that 993 has the phrase 'intueris quanto sublimis' inserted between the words 'propensius . . . esse'). The Gelasian (Vat. Reg. 316)[3] repro-duces 303 exactly except for the use of 'magisterio' in place of 'moderamine'. The Gregorian (Vat. Reg. 337),[4] Bobbio (Paris,

---

[1] The Roman prayers are preserved in the *Gelasian Sacramentary* (Vat. Reg. 316), and among the Gallican books in the *Missale Francorum* (Vat. Reg. 257).

[2] Cf. formulae 148–52: 322–6.

[3] Mohlberg, *Sacramentarium Gelasianum*, formula 921.

[4] *The Gregorian Sacramentary*, ed. Wilson, p. 87.

B.N. lat. 13246),[1] Missale Gothicum (Vat. Reg. 317),[2] and the Missale Romanum all reproduce this collect in roughly the same form as we first find it in the Leonianum. The first collect 280 is already what Jungmann[3] would describe as an 'amplified' type. The prayer is not the simplest of petitions: it has a number of ornaments and extra clauses, and in fact reads as a polished liturgical composition. The usual form of this 'amplified' type is 'Deus, qui . . .', the relative clause being an enlargement on the address 'Deus' and containing praise and adoration of the Godhead. In this case, however, it is enlarged by a phrase indicating that the feast of SS. Peter and Paul is being celebrated, and this is done by what is known as 'relative predication'—already a literary device in liturgical prayer, suitable and fitting for a gathering of the Christian community for its solemn address to God the Father. Particularly appropriate at this point is Jungmann's comment: 'The appearance of this amplified type in the collect is not governed by any strict rule, but we can say that this relative predication is generally found only on days of special solemnity, namely days of commemoration.'[3] In this respect the Gelasian, Gregorian, Bobbio, and Missale Romanum agree. On the other hand 303, 357, and the Missale Gothicum all employ extended, more florid forms of the address—'Omnipotens sempiterne Deus . . .'. The terse form of address, in which the prayer is directed simply to God ('Deus . . .'), is a probable indication that the prayer is an earlier recension than 303 and 357. 357 is the only collect which contains the term 'mysterio consecrasti'—each of the other collects reads 'martyrio consecrasti'. Further, between the words 'eorum' and 'per quos' 357 introduces the phrase 'sequi pia devotione doctrinam', where 280, 303, Gelasian, Bobbio, and the Missale Gothicum are agreed in using the phrase 'semper magisterio gubernari' (with slight changes in 303 and Bobbio), whilst the Gregorian and the Missale Romanum have the phrase 'in omnibus sequi preceptum'. These are the differences which are most striking when one looks at these eight collects side by side. In an attempt to show what the possible sources of these

---

[1] E. A. Lowe (ed.), *The Bobbio Missal* (Henry Bradshaw Society, London, 1920) p. 101 n. 329.

[2] Mohlberg, *Missale Gothicum*, formula 374.

[3] Op. cit., vol. i, p. 375.

various formulae may be, it is helpful to represent them in diagrammatic form:

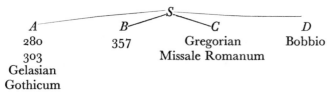

The columns A, B, C, D represent different sources which may or may not be related. Again the four formulae noted in column A may be from an independent source or they may be dependent upon one another in some way—the possibility of either is open.[1] In column A 280, 303, Gelasian, and Gothicum are all grouped together because, except for very minor verbal differences, the body of the collects is identical. 357 is placed by itself because it seems to embody different phrases, yet is generally built upon the plan of those in A. The Missale Romanum is identical in this collect with the Gregorian; it is obvious that the former has embodied the prayer of the latter, but the source of the Gregorian is again distinct from the others, so too is the Bobbio—yet the basic pattern of all the collects remains the same. It must be remembered that originally each of these formulae existed independently—or, if not entirely independently, then at least in very small groups on single pieces of parchment, which have come to be known as 'libelli'. The suggestion is that the compiler of the Leonianum selected his material from a large number of these single 'libelli'.[2]

We now pass on to a consideration of the structure of the collects themselves. They can be broken down into perfectly intelligible single phrases which may themselves have been in independent circulation, but we must leave this particular point for further discussion at a later stage. If 280 is taken as a representative collect then it is possible to see by its structure its relation to the others:

1. The opening address 'Deus'. (In 303, 357, and Missale Gothicum this has been extended to 'Omnipotens sempiterne Deus'.)

---

[1] Ultimately, of course, all must be related to one another in some way. It is impossible to imagine that two or more formulae for the most part identical could have been composed simultaneously in quite distinct centres.

[2] Bourque, op. cit., pp. 41–62.

2. By use of the relative 'qui' information is given about the feast day: 'qui hunc diem beatorum apostolorum Petri et Pauli martyrio consecrasti'.

3. Petition: 'da aeclesiae [tuae?]'.

4. Qualifying phrase of 'ecclesiae': 'toto terrarum orbe diffusae'.

5. Continuation of the petition (3): 'eorum semper magisterio gubernari'.

6. Further qualification of the apostles and the church: 'per quos sumpsit religionis exordium'. This forms the link between this particular regional church (in this case the Church of Rome) and the apostles Peter and Paul.

Leaving aside for a moment the minor differences in the phrases from collect to collect, each of these six parts occurs in every collect which has been noted here, except those which are taken from the Bobbio Missal and the Gregorian Sacramentary. In both cases the phrase 'toto terrarum orbe diffusa' is omitted as a qualification of 'ecclesia'. The collect is written for the commemoration both of St. Peter and St. Paul on the same day; some have maintained that this tradition is already evident by the time St. Clement is writing his first Epistle.[1] The Church of Rome, that is the regional Church, mindful of the witness of SS. Peter and Paul to their faith, prays that it may always be guided and governed by them, the founders of the See; such is the petition of the collect. It may be that as a prelude to the final formulation of the prayer there was the necessity to use phrases which had previously been used or, on the other hand, for the celebrant himself to construct them; certainly it was he who for the most part linked them together so that a complete prayer was formed. It seems likely that such phrases for use in liturgical compositions became set in a much more rigid form at an earlier stage than did the collect as a whole. A closer examination must be made of one phrase which is employed in the collect, 'toto terrarum orbe diffusa' as used in relation to 'ecclesia'. This appears to be a stereotyped phrase which the celebrant of the Eucharist has decided to employ in this particular collect. The phrase itself obviously qualifies the term 'ecclesia' and it seems to be the sort of phrase which is used almost without thought when the word 'ecclesia' occurs. Whilst he

---

[1] I Clement, v and vi.

does not use these exact words, the idea of the Church as diffused throughout the whole world is put forward for the first time in any serious treatise by Cyprian, Bishop of Carthage (d. A.D. 258), at a time when both the African and the Roman Churches found themselves attacked by the Novatianists, who themselves claimed to be the true Church. It is in order to clarify the issues, especially concerning the nature of the Church and its function, that Cyprian writes in his *De unitate ecclesiae*:[1]

sic et ecclesia domini luce perfusa per orbem totum radios suos porrigit; unum tamen lumen est quod ubique diffunditur, nec unitas corporis separatur. Ramos suos in universam terram copia uberitatis extendit, profluentes largiter rivos latius pandit: unum tamen caput est et origo una et una mater fecunditatis successibus copiosa: illius fetu nascimur, illius lacte nutrimur, spiritu eius animamur.

The work was probably written in May A.D. 251, about the time of the Carthaginian synod of that year. It is from *Ep.* 54. 4 that we learn that this work was certainly sent to Rome in the hope that it would bring about a reconciliation between the Novatianists and Pope Cornelius. Another bishop of the African Church, Optatus of Milevis (*c.* A.D. 370), whose penetrating arguments against the Donatists provided St. Augustine with the basis of his own refutation of this schism, himself speaks in very similar terms to Cyprian about the nature of the Church. Indeed in *De schismate Donatistarum*, vii. 2 is the exact phrase which is used in these collects:

probavimus, eam esse catholicam, quae sit in toto terrarum orbe diffusa.

Again in the *Contra Parmenianum*, ii. 12 the following passage occurs:

nam quis dubitet vos illud legitimum in sacramentum mysterio praeterire non posse? offerre vos Deo dicitis pro ecclesia quae una est. Hoc ipsum mendacii pars est unam te vocare de qua feceris duas: et offerre vos dicitis Deo pro una ecclesia quae sit in toto terrarum orbe diffusa.

Continuing in the tradition of the African Church, Augustine himself uses expressions almost identical with those found in

---

[1] Migne, *P.L.* 4. 517–18.

Optatus.[1] Obviously by the time Augustine was writing, the phrase was one commonly used when speaking of the Church and its universal appeal, as opposed to the schismatic Donatists. It must be remembered that throughout the whole of this period there was a great deal of communication between the Church in Africa and the Church in Rome. It would not be unnatural therefore to expect phrases which were in such common usage among the greatest writers of the African Church, and especially St. Augustine, whose influence upon the Church at large has been so tremendous, to appear again in the literary works of the Roman bishops. This is exactly what we find in the works of Pope Leo the Great—himself a staunch upholder of the importance and authority of the Roman See in its relation to the universal Church. He is very conscious of his position as a successor of the apostle Peter who, he contends, still presides and operates through the occupant of the chair of Peter. Leo's sermons resound with the praises of the apostle Peter and his guardianship over the See of Rome in his own episcopate. It is in the sermons of Leo that the phrase under discussion is to be found. Again in the context of 'ecclesia' we find

nam licet omnem ecclesiam, quae in toto est orbe terrarum, cunctis oporteat florere virtutibus, vos tamen praecipue inter caeteros populos decet mentis pietatis excellere, quos in ipsa apostolicae petrae arce fundatos, et Dominus noster Jesus Christus cum omnibus redemit.[2]

It is next used in relation to the joyous feast-day of the church of Rome itself, that of St. Peter.[3]

From this brief survey we can certainly say that the phrase itself was widely used with reference to the Church and that it had found its way into the liturgical prayer of the Church at

---

[1] He speaks of the prayer on behalf of the faithful which is made during the liturgy: *Ep.* xlix. 2 'quoniam ecclesiam Dei, quae catholica dicitur . . . per orbem terrarum diffusam videmus'; *Sermo* ccxliii 'interrogo ecclesiam toto orbe diffusam'; *Sermo* cclxvii 'ecce et haec unitas ecclesiae catholicae commendatur toto orbe diffusa' Further examples of Augustine's use of this phrase are to be found in *Ep.* xlix. 2, lii. 1, cxlii. 1, *Enarr. in Pss.* xxx. 2. 8, xlv. 1. 32, xc. 2. 1, *Sermo* ccxxxviii. 3.

[2] Leo, *Sermo* iii (Migne, *P.L.* 54. 147–8).

[3] Leo, *Sermo* lxxxii. 1 (Migne, *P.L.* 54. 422) 'verum tamen hodierna festivitas praeter illam reverentiam quam toto terrarum orbe promeruit'; *Sermo* lxxxiii. 1 (Migne, *P.L.* 54. 429) 'cuius hodierna solemnitas, recurrente triumpho matyrrii, specimen et decus contulit orbi terrarum'.

Rome. But, as has already been noted, the seed was first sown and indeed flourished in North Africa in the third and fourth centuries, and no doubt Augustine himself used it in his own liturgical compositions; after all the catholic Church's universality was its boast against the Donatists. It is certain then that we have here a non-Roman phrase used in a Roman prayer on one of the great festival days of the local Roman Church. But this is hardly surprising in view of the evidence suggesting so close a liaison between the Churches of Rome and North Africa.

After this survey of the particular forms of the collect for the feast-day of SS. Peter and Paul, there are several points to be noted. The stage has not yet been reached when the same prayer or set of prayers is prescribed for this same feast-day each year; some latitude still appears to be allowed in their composition. The formulation of much of the material in many of the various prayers and more especially the Eucharistic prayer itself was for a long time left to the celebrant of the Eucharist himself—he might extemporize to the best of his ability.[1] Origen in his 'Conversation with Heraclides'[2] rebukes some bishops for having introduced their own peculiar, possibly heretical, views into the prayer made at the Eucharistic offering. He is reported to have described the correct Eucharistic prayer. From this occasion it is clear that there were certain 'conventions' which the bishop was expected, though not compelled, to use in the composition of his prayer. Augustine himself provides evidence of the existence of both these methods of composition. He warns the well-educated catechumens not to mock at some of the rather crude, unpolished liturgical compositions of certain bishops.[3] At the synod of Hippo (A.D. 393) it was decided that only approved compositions were to be used:

quicumque sibi preces aliunde describit non eis utatur, nisi prius eas cum instructioribus fratribus contulerit.

The Leonianum itself generally reflects this situation as still obtaining in Rome during the fifth and sixth centuries. It seems

[1] Justin, *Apol.* i. 67. 5.
[2] *Entretien d'Origène avec Héraclide*, ed. J. Scherer (Cairo, 1949), pp. 129–30. Cf. R. P. C. Hanson, 'The Liberty of the Bishop to improvise prayer in the Eucharist', *Vigiliae Christianae*, 15 (1961), pp. 173–6.
[3] Augustine, *De Cat. Rud.* viii.

clear that what happened in the development of the Eucharistic prayer is almost exactly paralleled in the development of the collect. Obviously the Leonianum has reproduced more of the 'conventional' type of prayers for the sole reason that by this time the period of free composition is nearing its end, and liturgical formulae are beginning to crystallize into a more stereotyped form as a whole. At the same time there is evidence enough here for the existence of liturgical phrases and 'conventions' for use by those who were not so adept in their own compositions. It seems reasonable to conclude that, with the reduplication of collects, the period reflected by the Leonianum is one in which a new formula, or set of formulae, is composed for each celebration of the Eucharist; though, as we have seen, in any particular set of parallels the content of the formulae is so nearly similar that the time cannot be very long delayed before a single prayer is preserved and used on any particular feast-day. This would quite adequately explain the minor verbal differences of 280 and 303, where 280 reads 'magisterio gubernari' and 303 reads 'moderamine gubernari'.[1] It is almost impossible to say from this small point which is the earlier reading; Leo's sermons themselves demonstrate the interchangeability of such words as 'magisterium' and 'moderamen'.

Clearly then there is much which other liturgical books have in common with the Leonianum. Indeed, as we have seen, about two-thirds of the formulae of the present manuscript (which itself is incomplete) are to be found in other books, whilst one-third are peculiar to the Leonianum. It is highly unlikely that the formulae common to the Leonianum and other books should first have been incorporated into the Leonianum and from that manuscript passed into these books. This would be a similar theory to that which sees the Leonianum as the first in a series of official Roman sacramentaries; and these in their turn the prototypes of other liturgical books of Gallican and Celtic origin. In some examples which have been presented, the similarity between formulae has been absolute, in others extensive differences have occurred. Of the formulae in the Leonianum which do not occur in other books, many appear in the July group INCIPIUNT ORATIONES ET PRAECES DIURNAE; it is in this

---

[1] Clearly in the case of this set of parallel prayers the two words 'magisterio' and 'moderamine' are more likely to be scribal errors.

section that formulae reflecting a strong personal polemic occur most frequently, it is not surprising therefore that they are not to be found elsewhere. Undoubtedly, the many identical formulae in the different liturgical books are to be explained, in the beginning at least, by their origin in a common source. It is known that there were in existence at the Lateran many 'libelli missarum' from different sanctuaries in the city of Rome and the papal 'scrinium'. It is this collection (presumably available for those who wished to consult the 'libelli') which has produced the multiplicity of such prayers; though undoubtedly later in the eighth and ninth centuries copying from one book to another became a familiar feature.

11

THE NATURE AND PURPOSE OF
THE LEONINE SACRAMENTARY

T HE point has now been reached when consideration must be given to the collection as a whole. Whereas in the foregoing chapters attention has been directed to details within the Sacramentary, the attempt must now be made to discover precisely the nature of the collection and also the purpose of its compilation. In order to do this, we cannot be concerned merely with the contents of the book, though naturally these will be of considerable importance in any such consideration. Equally important will be an awareness of other liturgical manuscripts and what place the Leonine Sacramentary can be said to hold among them. Already in the chapter dealing with the problem of authorship and date, the rather tenuous connection between Pope Leo (as author of the complete collection) and the Sacramentary has been discarded; though it is not denied that he is responsible for some of the material contained therein. For the date of the actual manuscript reliance is placed upon the palaeographers, who assign it to some time about the year A.D. 600. If this be accepted, then from the dates proposed for certain sections of the Sacramentary there is little time between the composition of these sections as independent units and the Sacramentary as a whole. The study so far has raised many problems, still providing material for dispute. In the present chapter it is hoped that some more positive conclusions may be reached whereby a clearer picture may emerge of the Sacramentary—its material, its place of origin, and its position *vis-à-vis* other extant liturgical manuscripts.

A close examination of the 'sanctorale' in the Leonianum clearly leads to the conclusion that its list of saints can only have come from the Church of Rome. In addition to the commemoration of St. John Baptist, SS. John and Paul, SS. Peter and Paul, St. Laurence, SS. Hippolytus and Pontianus, SS. Adauctus and

Felix, SS. Cornelius and Cyprian, St. Euphemia, the Quattuor Coronati, St. Cecilia, SS. Clement and Felicity, and St. Andrew (all of which have been shown to have their origins in the local Roman Church), there are four titles that indicate even more clearly the connection between the commemoration of the saint's death and, if not the actual place of martyrdom, then at least the place where the saint was buried after death. Certainly the place of martyrdom has been an important consideration in the location of the feast of St. Xystus, who was in fact put to death in the catacombs of Callistus. In addition to the catacombs of Callistus those of Praetextatus are also mentioned. Situated on the Via Appia, these are the two most famous resting-places of saints and martyrs; the former containing the burial-place of many of the Roman bishops, Fabian, Eusebius, Stephen, Xystus, and Cornelius. Also mentioned in the title to group XVII, the cemeteries 'Maximi', 'Iornarum', and 'Priscillae' are situated on the Via Salaria, a branch road off the Via Nomentana and flowing in a northerly direction out of the city. On the Via Salaria the Basilica of S. Michael is to be found; the occasion of the dedication of this basilica is indicated by the title of formulae 844–57. The dedication of a further basilica, on this occasion to the apostle Peter, is to be found in the month of April. The formulae 130–3 are entitled 'In dedicatione'—it has been suggested that the situation of this basilica is some distance out of the city, along the Tiberine Way. The basilica itself was erected and dedicated in the early part of the sixth century. Names foreign to the local Roman Church are not found in the 'sanctorale' of the Leonianum. The list of names, at least in its present form, provides information for the second half of the year only. Evidence is lacking for any commemorations which may have taken place in the first half. The Sacramentary does, however, open with a section containing forty-three sets of formulae which from their content might well be described as a 'Common' of saints and/or confessors and/or martyrs. This portion of the Sacramentary is comparable to that of the 'Common of Paschaltide' in later manuscripts, but, except for set xxvi, there is nothing which is particularly indicative of the Paschal season. Most of the formulae mention 'martyrs', some 'martyrs and confessors', whilst 'confessors' only and 'saints' are to be found in but a few. The formulae 52–6 are for the commemoration of a female martyr, whilst the names Laurence (72), Tiburtius (2), and 'Gregori' (126) are the only proper names to occur in this whole section.

From the 'sanctorale' we pass now to a consideration of the remainder of the material within the Sacramentary. A detailed consideration has been given to the forty-five groups of formulae which, in the month of July, appear under the general heading INCIPIUNT ORATIONES ET PRAECES DIURNAE. A large number of the formulae undoubtedly reflect troubled times, both civil and ecclesiastical. During the greater part of the fifth and sixth centuries the whole of Italy became the scene of hostile encounters between the Italian populace and the invading Arian marauders. As a study of certain formulae in an earlier chapter has shown, the political situation and the condition of the people during the time of war have not escaped the liturgical prayer of the Church. The particular connection with the city of Rome, and possibly more particularly with the sieges of that city by Alaric, Genseric, Ricimer, and Vitiges, and the conditions and reactions of the citizens in such a state are clearly reflected by a number of these prayers. Chavasse particularly has endeavoured to show that a large number of the forty-five sets of the July group belong to the troubled years A.D. 537 and 538. In addition to the troubles in the country itself, the Church also appears to have been beset with intrigue and embroilment. Following for the most part the arguments of Bourque, the most likely context to which these sets of formulae are to be ascribed is the period of strife and revolt towards the end of the Laurentian schism (A.D. 502–6). The intense subjectivity of some of the proper prefaces within this section illustrates effectively the personal struggle between two men which was ultimately the cause of so much strife within the Church. However, the factor which is common to both civil and ecclesiastical turmoil, so far as our formulae are concerned, is that they reflect these conditions in one particular centre, and clearly that centre is Rome. In fact throughout the Sacramentary there are a number of formulae which mention the city by name: 218, 292, 307, 361, 480, 553, 590, 604, 605, 660, 779, 872, 1128, 1132.

In spite of the fact that there is disagreement about the actual date to which the various sets entitled 'In natale episcoporum' should be assigned, it is not a point of dispute that their place of origin is the city of Rome. The bishop whose celebration it is is the occupant of the chair of the apostle Peter—this is made explicit in the text (cf. 989).

Undoubtedly the text of the Sacramentary gives the impression that it is Roman in origin. There is no group of formulae with particularly marked characteristics which would indicate that their place of origin is to be sought elsewhere. The prayers of the Mass, at least those found in the Leonianum—the collect, secret prayer (at the offertory), proper preface, and post-communion—have still not reached an entirely fixed form; that is, a set of prayers fixed for use on any particular day in the year, be it Sunday or feast-day. In such a situation it would not be surprising to find the existence of a large number of 'libelli'— sets of Mass formulae or groups of sets, brought together and preserved in some central place. The Lateran became such a centre for the compositions of the Roman bishops and no doubt for the compositions used in the local churches and cemeteries. The contents of the Leonianum itself reflect the existence of a large number of sets of Mass prayers for any one feast. Indeed on 10 July, the feast of the Seven Brothers, three separate Eucharists may possibly have been celebrated: one 'ad Aquilorem', in the catacombs of Praetextatus on the Via Appia for Januarius; one 'ad Alexandrum' for Alexander, Vitalis, and Martial 'in Iornarum', also for Felix and Philip in the neighbouring cemetery 'Priscillae' on the Via Salaria; and the third 'ad St. Felicitatem' in the cemetery 'Maximi' for Silanus. Since the formulae for this feast in the Leonianum are all of a general nature, making no mention of individual martyrs, it is possible that three copies of one set of formulae would have sufficed for the three separate commemorations; or there may have been slight variations at each of the three celebrations in order to establish more closely the connection with the particular saint. Again, on the feast of SS. Peter and Paul, it is possible that two celebrations could have taken place, the one at the Vatican, the other on the Via Ostiensis.[1] No doubt the formulae would have been varied in view of the particular connection with an apostle at each of the two supposed burial-sites.

[1] The possibility of a double commemoration at the shrine on the Via Appia must also be reckoned with.

The large number of sets of formulae which are to be found attached to particular feast-days (St. John Baptist, 5; SS. John and Paul, 8; St. Laurence, 14) are undoubtedly indicative of the existence of many such sets, composed for the particular day in the year and then preserved. It may be that some of the similarities in the text of formulae within the Leonianum (e.g. where part of a collect of one set is to be found in a proper preface of another set) can be explained in this way, i.e. that a set of formulae used one year, already preserved, is consulted, and perhaps parts of this set incorporated, in order to make up the set for the following year; though clearly it was not a necessity to consult or use previous compositions.

It would seem intrinsically possible then that the collection of 'libelli', the product of the local Roman churches and cemeteries, was preserved at the Lateran, the residence of the bishop of Rome from the fourth century onwards; and that it is from this collection that the material in the Leonianum was largely derived. Having made this assertion, we are now faced with a much more vexed question. Is the manuscript also of Roman origin? In view of the paucity of evidence for either a positive or negative answer to be given on this point, the question has naturally provoked much discussion. There is in fact no external evidence whatever of the existence or use of the manuscript in Rome. Moreover, there is similarly no external evidence of its existence or use in any other centre. An examination of the manuscript itself has led us to conclude that it has quite definite connections with Verona by the late eighth century. But, since the palaeographers give the manuscript a date about the eary A.D. 600, it follows that for one hundred and fifty years or more the history of the manuscript lies hidden in obscurity. Certain more positive facts, however, do emerge from a study of the manuscript which would tend to suggest Verona as its place of origin. The continuation of the liturgical text on fol. 139, in different ink and in a different hand from the rest of the Sacramentary, is suggested by Lowe to have been executed in the seventh century.[1] The mixed uncial and half-uncial script in which the continuation is written has close similarities with other manuscripts to be found among the Verona collection and which are North Italian in origin. Further, the script in which

---

[1] Lowe, op. cit. iv, p. 32 n. 514.

most of the marginal notes are written is cursive and certainly of North Italian origin also; the Veronese origin of such script is less certain. The palaeographic evidence concerning the origin and existence of the manuscript is certainly much more indicative of a North Italian centre than Rome; for in spite of the fact that there is no external evidence for the manuscript's existence or use in any centre, the internal evidence of the manuscript itself, its script and marginal notes, points to North Italy. There is much to commend Lowe's argument at this point.[1] Since there is no palaeographical evidence to the contrary, and since the manuscript has existed at Verona from the eighth century at least (this is the earliest date at which we can be quite certain of its connection with this centre), and since it exhibits no definite characteristics of manuscripts from other centres, then the presumption is that the manuscript originated in Verona. It cannot, however, be said that the Veronese origin of the manuscript is proved. In any case, for such evidence as there is, we are dependent upon the palaeographers, who themselves have drawn widely differing conclusions: De Beer suggests an origin in Spain; Traube, Africa; Bishop, possibly Bobbio; and Cabrol, Africa. It is interesting to note that Rome, as the place of origin of the manuscript, does not have a place among the suggestions made. Bischoff is content with the statement 'außerhalb Roms (in Verona?) zusammengestellt'.[2] In view of the uncertainty presented by the evidence this is a commendable, if rather sceptical, position to take. However, considering points in the study of the manuscript, made earlier, the suggestion of Verona as the place of origin is certainly not out of keeping with the known evidence.

A further difficulty now appears. It has been established that the contents of the Leonianum are almost exclusively Roman, yet whether we accept Verona or some other centre, it is extremely unlikely that Rome is the place of origin of the actual manuscript. In other words, the Leonianum is a book containing Roman material yet written in a non-Roman centre. The conclusion is: either that the compiler has had access to Roman material in a centre other than Rome itself, or that he has made a visit to Rome and copied out various of the 'libelli'

[1] Lowe, op cit. iv, p 32 n. 514.
[2] B. Bischoff in K. Gamber, 'Sakramentartypen', p. 48.

from which our manuscript has been produced. The latter is more likely to be correct, since there is no evidence that material such as is found in the Sacramentary ever existed at any centre other than Rome, where clearly material such as the Sacramentary contains would abound. Following this point, it may be well to ask exactly what relevance some of the formulae would have in a church which is not to be found in Rome itself—the formulae so rich in reference to Rome, the Roman Church, the Roman people, and the Roman saints and martyrs. We must also note the very erratic method of arrangement (which is the cause of a number of misplaced formulae), and must recognize the existence in the July section of the Sacramentary of fierce attacks upon personal adversaries.[1] Consequently, it is here suggested that the Leonianum is not a sacramentary (i.e. an official collection of prayers for use at Mass) in the accepted sense of the word, and that it was never used or intended for use in a church. Rather it is a purely private collection, the result of some unknown person's antiquarian, historical, liturgical interests. In support of this Lowe suggests that the informal uncial script in which the book is written is unusual in liturgical documents. (But what other 'liturgical documents' are there at this date with which the Leonianum can be compared?) Others would disagree with this, maintaining that the script, which is quite large and not difficult to read, would favour the use of the Leonianum in church, and that it was in fact compiled for this purpose. Having inspected the manuscript, the present writer would certainly agree about the legibility of the script; and, further, would point out that the addition of the red colour to certain of the titles, sub-titles, marginal numbers, and paragraph markings would make the handling of the compilation much easier for any celebrant. Without the distinctive red markings it would be extremely difficult to find any particular set of prayers. Thus there is nothing about the manuscript itself which would necessarily preclude its being used in church, though there is no evidence by which we could wholly accept or reject such a view. It is an examination of the material which will no doubt lead one to

---

[1] Especially the proper preface 530.

[2] e.g. the titles (in red) 'In natale Sanctorum Iohannis et Pauli' and 'In natale Apostolorum Petri et Pauli'.

sympathize with those who assert that the Leonianum is a purely private venture. It is impossible to conceive that those prayers, which, it has been suggested, were composed for some particular event in the life of the Roman people, were used among any other community than that of Rome itself. Also the sets of Mass formulae for use on the anniversary of an episcopal ordination seem to presuppose the bishop of Rome. One of the proper prefaces assigned to the feast day of SS. John and Paul assumes that the celebrant is at Rome and in the church dedicated to the two martyrs.[1] So do many of the formulae of the Masses for the feast of SS. Peter and Paul. Also in the section of Requiem formulae several appear to take it for granted that those present are at the Roman city church of St. Laurence and that the Eucharist is being offered for one of the bishops of Rome who lies buried within the walls of that church.[2] At the same time it is true that there are a large number of formulae, more general in application, which could well be used in any area, but this would still not explain the existence of so many prayers which could only be properly used in Rome itself. Duchesne, Muratori, and others have argued that the existence in the July section of proper prefaces which exhibit a crudely polemic content could not possibly find a place in any official Sacramentary. But it is not wholly legitimate to use these prefaces to support such an argument. Rather are they reflections of a period when liturgical prayer was very much less formal and much more left to the discretion of the celebrant. With Duchesne[3] it must be agreed that the compiler could hardly have invented such strange prefaces. But their presence is not necessarily indicative of the fact that this is only a private collection; though by the year A.D. 600 (the date of our manuscript) liturgical prayer would be in the process of becoming much more formal and stereotyped in its phraseology. Unless the Leonianum is regarded as a purely private venture,[4] the existence of such strong Roman elements in a centre other than Rome is very difficult to explain.

---

[1] Formula 271.
[2] Formulae 1151, 1152, and 1155.
[3] L. Duchesne, *Christian Worship*, p. 143.
[4] This does not involve passing any opinion as to whether it was used in any church outside Rome at some later stage; this has been established as a possibility, though there is no evidence that it ever was.

Is it possible then to regard the Leonianum as a sacramentary? By its very nature a sacramentary is a book used by a celebrant in which could be found all the parts of the Mass which he has to recite—the collect, secret prayer (offertory), proper preface, Canon, and post-communion. Except the Canon, which does not appear in our present manuscript, all the other elements are present. Much speculation has taken place in regard to the Canon; whether in fact it was originally part of the book. Though the question is interesting and open to discussion, there is no evidence which would support or deny the existence of the Canon in the part of the manuscript now lost. Until the missing fragment is recovered, if it ever is, such questions must of necessity remain open and unanswered. In other respects the Leonianum would be consonant with the description of a sacramentary given above, if such a description did not imply that the composition of the book was made with the intention of its being used in a particular church. However, it can be said that the Leonianum is a sacramentary in so far as it is a collection of formulae such as have been mentioned above, but that it is not strictly 'liturgical' since, in the first instance, it is a private composition. Certainly it cannot be regarded as a sacramentary in the same way as the Gelasian or Gregorian. Moreover, from a survey of extant manuscripts there is no evidence of the existence, about the year A.D. 600, of other sacramentaries. Indeed it is only in the latter half of the eighth century that books similar to Vat. Reg. 316 (c. A.D. 750), Angoulême (B.N. Lat. 816—c. A.D. 800), St. Gall 348 (c. A.D. 800) make an appearance at all. From the date of the composition of the Leonianum (c. A.D. 600) until the appearance of these manuscripts the evidence points to the existence of fragments such as the Masses of Mone (7th century), the Ravenna Rotulus (c. A.D. 700), the Cambridge Fragment at Gonville and Caius (c. A.D. 750), the Merton Fragment at Slindon[1] (c. A.D. 750), and also fuller collections of formulae, not yet completely developed in the form and structure exhibited in the Gelasian and Gregorian—the Stowe Missal,[2] the

[1] The present whereabouts of this manuscript is obscure—it has been sold privately.

[2] This is dated variously from the sixth to the eighth century, but a date towards the end of the eighth century appears to be more generally accepted. If the 'Maileruen' of the diptychs is taken to indicate St. Maelruain of Tallaght then the text must be later than A.D. 792, the date of his death. For a fuller discussion of this

Missale Gothicum (c. A.D. 700), and the Bobbio Missal (c. A.D. 700). It is only when the late eighth century is reached that there emerges the fully developed form of the sacramentary; this is evident from the profusion of manuscripts of Gelasian- and Gregorian-type sacramentaries of this and the following century. From a survey, then, of the liturgical manuscripts from the sixth to the ninth centuries, it becomes clear that the Leonianum is an isolated example of such a collection of Mass formulae, as early as the year A.D. 600. Even the evidence of similar manuscripts at the beginning of the eighth century points only to small fragmentary collections; certainly there are no collections so full as the Leonianum until the mid eighth century is reached. This feature would possibly favour those who maintain that the Leonianum is but a collection made privately, since it is the only manuscript of its kind at that date.

It is true that this fact has been questioned. E. Bishop[1] wrote: 'The Verona Leonianum is clearly not a "unicum" for the Gallican Missals—the Gothicum, Gallicanum (Bobbio), Francorum, all draw, and draw freely, from this collection, which, it is evident, must have been, as a document or collection, once widely spread on this side of the Alps.' But against this Bourque[2] concludes: 'Le manuscrit 85 de Vérone est, de fait, un "unicum".' It is true that the Gothicum, Bobbiense, and Francorum all have certain formulae in common with the Leonianum. But can it be said that they 'draw, and draw freely, from this collection'? It is certainly an exaggeration to say that they drew freely upon the Leonianum. Indeed it may be asked if they drew upon this document at all. The Gothicum may have 87 formulae or parts of formulae in common with the Leonianum, the Bobbiense 31, and the Francorum 45. But when it is considered that the Leonianum contains 1331 formulae, it is hardly accurate to say that these compositions have 'drawn freely' upon our document. Again many of the formulae which these books have in common cannot be said to follow one another absolutely verbatim. As has been argued previously, is not the

point, see *The Stowe Missal*, vol. ii (ed. G. F. Warner, H.B.S., London, 1915), especially Introduction, pp. xxxii ff.; also F. E. Warren, *The Liturgy and Ritual of the Celtic Church*, pp. 198–268.

[1] E. Bishop, op. cit., 1918, p. 197.
[2] Bourque, op. cit., pp. 155–7.

existence of similar formulae in other books to be attributed to their each having consulted a common source, viz. the Roman 'libelli' which were copied by visitors to that city and carried back to their native parts, and in the case of such Gallican compositions, added to the already existing liturgical prayers proper to their own areas? Also it must be noted that never is there to be found in other liturgical books a whole set of Mass formulae which are exactly similar to those in the Leonianum. The parallels are isolated and confined to the odd formula here and there. Dom Gregory Dix[1] too makes the surprising statement: 'We know that other copies existed and were not confined to Italy.' But where is the evidence for such a statement? From a survey of the available evidence it would appear that support for such a statement is lacking. No other copy, either complete or fragmentary, of such a manuscript as the Leonianum has yet been discovered, nor is there any evidence of the existence of such copies in the catalogues of the great monastic libraries. Mention is certainly made in such catalogues of the Gelasian- and Gregorian-type sacramentaries.[2]

In view of the lack of evidence in support of the existence of other copies of the Leonianum, we must conclude, with Bourque, that the Verona manuscript is a 'unicum'. As we have already seen, it is not necessary to postulate the existence of other copies of this particular manuscript in order to explain the parallels in other books. Whether the manuscript is the archetype is again a difficult problem; in view of the confused order of the material and the large number of marginal and other notes Bourque[3] suggests that it is. Others have suggested that our present manuscript is a fair copy of material first gathered in Rome towards the middle of the sixth century. As the possibility of the manuscript's having originated in Verona has been established as fairly strong, and as much of the material is Roman, then the compiler must have made rough notes, at least, of the formulae which he found in Rome and, having returned home, made a fair copy which we know as Verona lxxxv (80). Even in the copying out of the rough notes such as were made in Rome it is still possible for material to be misplaced and thus necessitate

---

[1] G. Dix, *The Shape of the Liturgy*, p. 567.
[2] Cf. E. Bishop, op. cit., pp. 47 ff.
[3] Bourque, op. cit., pp. 154–5.

the insertion of marginal notes. Indeed we have already noted, in the description of the manuscript, the fact that the compiler, having completed the whole book, has looked over his work and at this stage made several insertions and corrections. Nevertheless, no attempt is made at correcting the blatant misplacement of the nine sets of Mass prayers for the feast of St. Stephen, proto-martyr.

Let us then retrace our conclusions. Because this particular period in the history of the development of the Roman Rite cannot be clearly or easily traced, our conclusions regarding the Leonine Sacramentary must necessarily remain to some extent tentative and unresolved. It has become clear that almost all the material within the Sacramentary has its origin in Rome. Not only the many explicit references to the city itself, but also the form and content of many of the prayers themselves are indicative of this view. But although it may be concluded that the material within the Sacramentary is Roman, nevertheless the centre in which the manuscript was written is still the subject of much debate. Since no evidence has been found which would support such a view, we have rejected Rome as that centre. The palaeographers also have always suggested some centre other than Rome. Rather the long connection with Verona has led us to conclude that this was the centre where the manuscript was written. Thus we have a collection of Roman material (much of which would be entirely unsuitable for use in any other centre) written, it is suggested, in Verona. The possibility of the collection's being used in a church in Verona is very slight indeed. The suggestion, therefore, is that in the first place the Leonine Sacramentary was a purely private collection; though, as we have seen, there is no clear evidence which would exclude the possibility of its subsequent use for the public worship of any particular Christian community. It is unlikely, then, that the Sacramentary ever had any official standing; it was certainly never, at any period, the obligatory standard text of the Roman Church. Whilst it may be agreed that the collection reflects much that is of interest and importance for the development of the liturgy in Rome during the fourth to the sixth centuries, the Leonine Sacramentary should never be viewed as the authoritative book in use at Rome during any particular period. With this in mind the concept of the Leonine as the first of a series of official Mass books put out by Rome can be dispelled. Since no evidence has been forthcoming of the existence of other copies of the book, it has been concluded, with Bourque, that our manuscript is a 'unicum'. The formulae which this book has in common with later liturgical documents we have attributed, for the most part, to a common source. Clearly much remains unresolved and uncertain. Whilst the Leonianum is one of the most interesting books for the study of the early liturgy it is also one of the most elusive. It has provided both the Roman Missal and the Book of Common Prayer with liturgical formulae which are distinctive for their 'simplicity, practicality, great sobriety and self-control, clarity and dignity'. These are words which Edmund Bishop[1] used to describe the early Roman rite as a whole; for this was its merit and its genius.

[1] E. Bishop, op. cit., p. 12.

ON SOME OF THE MARGINAL NOTES
IN THE SACRAMENTARY

THE marginal annotations which are our concern here and the places where they occur in the text are as follows:

1. Among the Masses which have been suggested as Commons of saints/martyrs/confessors:

(a) Paschalis (E?) F SP (Feltoe reads: Paschalis SC F SP). The letter or letters immediately after the word 'Paschalis' are impossible to distinguish clearly; but certainly the other two are F SP. The note appears just before the proper preface 96.

2. Among the Masses for the Feast of Pentecost (Group XI):

(b) Praece SF: between the two formulae 222 and 223.

3. Among the Masses for the Feast of SS. Peter and Paul (Group XV):

(c) F E: before the collect 303, in red in the right-hand-side margin.

(d) F E SP: after the preface 308 entitled 'Post Infirmitate'.

(e) F E SP: between the formulae 331 and 332.

(f) F E SP: just after the formula 336.

(g) P SP F E: after the second (358) of the two formulae which make up this set.

(h) P F E SP: after the formula 367.

4. Among the Masses entitled 'Incipiunt Orationes et Praeces Diurnae' (Group XVIII):

(i) P S F E: between the formulae 551 and 552.

(j) P F E SP: between the formulae 555 and 556.

(k) P F E SP: after a secret prayer (575) with no further formula in that set.

(l) P F E: between the two formulae 595 and 596.

(m) P F E: after the sixth formula (603) of set xxxiii.

The Veronensis lxxxv (80) contains the above-mentioned thirteen very abbreviated notes, which we have lettered (a) to (m). Their

L

meaning is obscure and still remains unsolved. Though these notes occur in the text in what seems to be quite an arbitrary fashion, yet the way in which they appear in the manuscript—the same script in which they are all written—seems to suggest that there is some basic purpose and method common to all. Not surprisingly, these very elusive markings have exercised many minds and it is the object of this note to outline the chief methods of interpretation, to comment briefly on these, and to assess their respective merits. The theories propounded have generally been based upon one of the following three main lines of interpretation:

1. That the notes serve to indicate the nature of the formula immediately following them, e.g. whether it is an offertory prayer, a post-communion, or a 'super populum' prayer. The chief supporters of this type of theory have been Bianchini and Probst.

2. That the notes were already part of the original 'libelli' from which the sets of formulae were drawn, and that it is within this context that an explanation must be sought. Dom R. H. Connolly has presented the arguments in favour of this view.

3. That the notes are a form of shorthand used by the compiler for indicating the point at which a formula is missing from any particular set. The notes themselves are taken to provide the clue to the missing formula. They refer us either to a formula which has already appeared within the text of the manuscript itself (this line of argument is followed by Buchwald, Andrieu, and Mohlberg), or to a formula contained in other material which the compiler had in hand (perhaps, for example, his own draft copy of the text). Feltoe and the palaeographer Lowe are the chief exponents of this view.

Thus having set out the various possibilities of approach, we must proceed to a fuller exposition of the views of those who have been named above.

I

One attempted interpretation of these signs occurs in the copy of Anastasius Bibliothecarius, *Vitae Romanorum Pontificum* in the Capitular Library at Verona.[1] A modern scribe has inserted in the margins of this copy the following solution: 'Praece sf (Praeces super fratres sine preces spiritui fienda); f e sp (facta eucharistia super populum) [here Bianchini suggests 'preces feriales']; p sp f e (preces super populum facta eucharistia); p f e sp (preces facta eucharistia super populum); p s f e (post sumptionem facta eucharistia); p f e sp (post

---

[1] Feltoe, op. cit., Introduction, p. x.

factam eucharistiam super populum); P F E (preces facta eucharistia).'

Over a hundred years later Probst[1] interpreted these signs in
a way very similar to that which had already been hinted at by
Bianchini:

Paschali SC F SP = 'Paschale sursum corda feriale super populum'
P F E SP = 'Preces feriales eiusdem super populum'

The remainder he took to be variants of the latter abbreviated note.

The main point about the two solutions just mentioned is that they
attempt to interpret the signs in terms of their particular context, i.e.
the set of formulae within which they are to be found. It matters
little whether they were to be found in the sources from which the
present forms have been taken or whether they were added by the
compiler. They are taken to be explanatory notes and are to be seen
in terms of the formulae within which they occur.

2

It is clear that the note PCES H IN SCE EUFYMIAE, which occurs just
before the proper preface 826, indicates that this preface belongs,
not to the set in which it appears in the Sacramentary (namely for
the feast of SS. Cornelius and Cyprian) but in the next group, for the
feast of St. Euphemia. Dom Connolly[2] maintains that this note has
none of the characteristics of the notes with which we are now concerned and does not help to explain them. He finds it difficult to
believe that these notes originated from the hand of the compiler of
the collection; rather he considers the only alternative would seem
to be that they were attached to certain groups of formulae when
these came into the hands of our compiler. Having first established
that, in the sermons of Pope Leo particularly, notices concerning the
religious observances for the coming week were given out at the
beginning, and that such notices were given out by way of a fairly
uniform formula, he then goes on to suggest that the notes in the
Leonianum are nothing more than short memoranda of such notices,
which were to be given out during the course of the Eucharist. He
observes that seven of the 'notae' begin with the letter P, and eight
contain the same letter P, whilst FE occurs in all but two of them.
Taking those notes, (g) to (k) in our list, which display these letters,
he suggests that these amount basically to the same thing, and can
be interpreted in the following way: P = 'processio' (in the fifth century used of any public celebration in church and particularly of the

---

[1] Probst, op. cit., pp. 109 f.
[2] H. Connolly, O.S.B., 'On some of the "notae" in the Leonine Sacramentary',
Revue bénédictine 38 (1926), pp. 196–204.

Eucharist), F E = 'futura est' and sp = '(ad/apud) S. Petrum'. Thus
the notice reads 'Processio futura est (ad/apud) S. Petrum'. The
remaining notes, without sp or p, he takes to be variants on the
others. One point is considered certain, that they are merely variations: if the clue to one such set of letters is found then the clue to the
whole series has been found—in longer or shorter form, they all say
the same thing. Thus, 'processio' would be taken to be understood,
not needing to be indicated in every case; also '(ad/apud) Sanctum
Petrum', the place where the celebration was to take place, might
similarly be taken for granted. Hence Dom Connolly interprets these
signs as abbreviated notices to be given out at the (presumably
Sunday) Eucharist of future celebrations and the place where such
celebrations would occur.

<h1 style="text-align:center">3</h1>

It was Buchwald who observed that several of the signs, especially
those beginning with the letter p, occurred in sets of formulae which
lacked a preface. This p he took to indicate 'Praece(s)', as in the note
following formula 222. The term 'preces' he interpreted as a reference to the Canon of the Mass ('prex' as used by St. Gregory) and
particularly to the preface with which the Canon begins. Thus the
notes in general refer the reader back to an earlier place in the manuscript for the missing formula. He proposes the following interpretations:

Paschali sc F sp = 'Paschalis secreta folii superior'
P F E sp= 'Preces folii eiusdem superiores'

Whilst we have seen that Connolly maintains that the insertion
PCES H IN SCE EUFYMIAE (820) is of no help when we come to consider
the abbreviated notes now under discussion, Andrieu[1] sees in such a
note the very basis of an explanation of the remaining notes. His
argument in fact begins with the inserted note PCES H IN SCAE
EUFYMIAE, which clearly establishes that this particular formula (a
proper preface in this case) has been misplaced (it occurs in the group
of formulae for the feast of SS. Cornelius and Cyprian) and that its
proper place is among the formulae for the feast of St. Euphemia.
Two points are deduced from this: (a) that the compiler (or possibly
a later hand) can, in this way, refer to something which occurs elsewhere in the book; and (b) that he can do this by brief notes or signs
such as these, which indicate where the prayers should properly be
placed. Like Buchwald, Andrieu considers it no mere coincidence

[1] M. Andrieu, 'Les sigles du sacramentaire léonien', *Revue bénédictine*, 42 (1930),
pp. 127–35.

that of the forty-five sets of formulae entitled INC ORATIONES ET PRAECES DIURNAE there are only five which do not have a proper preface (24, 25, 29, 32, 33) and that at the very place where the preface should be, i.e. after the secret prayer, a group of letters appears, of which the first is always P. In addition no other sets of formulae within this section contain such abbreviations. The conclusion is that there is some relation between the absence of a proper preface in five sets of formulae and, at the place where such formulae should occur, the appearance of these groups of letters. Hence the following interpretation:

P S F E (following 551): 'Prex (proper preface) supra (or superior) facienda est'. Or merely 'prex supra facta est', the preface is to be found above.

P F E (following 595): 'Prex facienda est', the celebrant must make up his own preface which occurs here. Or merely 'prex facta est', the preface to be used here has already been written.

Again, in group XV, entitled IN N APOSTOLORUM PETRI ET PAULI, out of twenty-eight sets of prayers there is only one without a proper preface (357–8), and again the same explanation of the letters P SP F E would seem to apply here, i.e. 'prex supra facta est'.

Thus in every case where the letter P has appeared initially it has been taken by Andrieu as an indication of the word 'prex' or 'prece' by which he understands 'proper preface'. But what of the set xxv, where the letters P F E SP all appear and yet there is also the proper preface 369 in the same set? Andrieu answers negatively and suggests there is an error here on the part of the compiler. The formula 367 'Apostolorum tuorum praecibus, domine...' is a secret prayer and not a collect, as Connolly and Mohlberg also assert. Indeed, in support of Andrieu it might be pointed out that virtually the same formula is to be found in Mass ii (248) used as a secret prayer; it is used in this manner in the Missale Romanum today. Following this secret prayer then (367) there are the letters P F E SP where the proper preface should be; there then follows another secret prayer 'Hostias, domine, quas nomini tuo...' (368) and a proper preface (369). Thus, it is suggested, there are here, under the one 'Item alia', the remains of two Masses, the first of which has been deprived of its proper preface. Andrieu suggests that it is for this reason that the two have been brought together to make up the one set.

There are, however, five further sets of formulae in which other signs appear; these do not contain the letter P among the other letters; none of the Masses is without a preface. The sign F E SP appears three times in such circumstances, immediately after 308, 331, and 336. In order to explain this symbol, Andrieu has to suppose a situation earlier than the collection, whilst the various elements were still fairly liquid, and suggests that Mass xi had been placed after Mass xiii. In this event the signs F E SP (i.e. this preface has already appeared above) would clearly point the reader to what has already been written out once before. Similar signs appear at the end of Mass xvi and Mass xvii. In the case of Mass xvi the letters appear after the formula 331; there is a parallel here with 371 and again Andrieu has to propose that originally the two sets of formulae were inverted so that the F E SP of Mass xvi can refer to the parallel formula in Mass xxv. He does not, however, have to resort to such an explanation for the appearance of these words after the formula 336 of Mass xvii, since the prayer, or at least part of it, has appeared earlier in formula 268. The simple sign F E, in red in the margin, appears just before the formula 303. The suggestion here is that this is merely an abbreviated form of F E SP—in other words, the prayer has been used before; indeed it is one of the parallels to that with which the group opens (280). The point which Andrieu makes about the phrase 'Paschalis E F SP' (between 95 and 96) is that it is to be interpreted as 'paschalis est, facta superius'; the preface 96 is one proper to the Paschal season, a parallel of which, he suggests, was to be found among the formulae of the part of the manuscript now missing. Unfortunately this statement cannot be verified.

Like Connolly, Andrieu finds it necessary to preserve the unity of these signs; they are all abbreviations which virtually say the same thing. In a work destined for public use, Andrieu finds it incomprehensible that such signs should occur without any explanation. Rather are they rapid annotations, made in the margins of the text by the compiler of the collection; this proposition he finds intelligible.

From the palaeographer's point of view, Lowe[1] remarks that these signs may possibly be seen as cross-references to the archetype.

Having surveyed the suggestions of scholars who have offered explanations of these notes, we must now attempt to assess the virtues and defects of their theories.

Because, like Andrieu, Probst and Buchwald based their hypotheses concerning these signs on the assumption that they are to be interpreted with regard to the arrangement of material in the manuscript, Connolly, by virtue of his own presuppositions, is forced to reject them. He writes: 'It cannot be said that they carry conviction, they are far-fetched, and really non-sensical.' He objects to such interpretations on three counts:

[1] Lowe, op. cit., no. 514.

(a) The set of formulae 367–71 contains the signs P F E SP (immediately after formula 367), yet it has a proper preface (369) and in all other respects is complete. However, as has been noted, Andrieu has provided at least one explanation of this anomaly.

(b) Two other sets of formulae (327–31; 332–6) each contain the note F E SP and yet appear to be complete.

(c) Throughout the book there are many other sets of formulae which, in various ways, are incomplete yet no such notes have been attached to them.

Thus Connolly concludes that Buchwald's suggestions are no more convincing than those of Probst.

It is clear, however, that Connolly's own theory stands or falls by its basic assumption, i.e. that these abbreviations were already to be found in the 'libelli' from which our compiler has taken much of his material. A close examination of the manuscript and the location of these notes in the manuscript renders such an assumption very uncertain.[1] It may, however, be more likely that the compiler himself is responsible for the insertion of such notes and that they are related in some way to the material within the Sacramentary. It is precisely this point which Andrieu takes up and thus provides what in many ways would seem to be a more satisfactory theory.

But before any further assessment is made, three preliminary points are perhaps worthy of note; these come from the present writer's examination of the manuscript:

(i) Can we really class the notes which appears in the left-hand-side margin, in red, at the side of formula 303, in the same category as the rest of the notes? This particular sign is written directly beneath the number viiii; even if we accept the first letter as F, it is very difficult to conclude that the second is E—certainly it does not have the same appearance as similar letters in other such notes.

(ii) Feltoe[2] prints the last formula 331 'Adesto, domine, fidelibus...' of set xvi of group XV; following this there are the letters F E SP. Mohlberg,[3] however, prints these same letters (F E SP) between ITEM ALIA and the opening words 'Omnipotens sempiterne deus . . .' of formula 332 at the beginning of set xvii. In a way both could be said to be correct. The position of the letters in the manuscript leaves both

---

[1] In any case, if these abbreviations are to be interpreted as notices of forthcoming Eucharistic celebrations, then at least we might expect some consistency as to the place in which they appear in the text.

[2] Feltoe, op. cit., p. 44, l. 9.

[3] L. C. Mohlberg, O.S.B., *Sacramentarium Veronense* (Rome, 1956), p. 45.

lines of interpretation open as a possibility. The part of the lines of the manuscript in question reads:

> . . . gloriosa confessio p. ITEM ALIA F E SP
> Omnipotens sempiterne . . .

Thus there is the preliminary task of making the decision as to whether these letters should be attached to formula 331 or 332.

(iii) The P SP F E attached to prayer 358 is written in the right-hand-side margin in smaller script more akin to that of the marginal notes by the side of certain other proper prefaces and certainly looks as if it has been added, possibly by the compiler himself as an after-thought, when the composition of the work was completed.

It may, however, be agreed with those who have attempted to provide a solution that all these signs can be regarded as indicating the same thing, though some are more abbreviated than others. They are to be taken as a unity. The really fundamental issue which must be settled before any decision can be made as to their meaning is one which has been mentioned briefly already. Did the signs form an original part of the 'libelli' used by our compiler or are they, in fact, the insertions of the compiler himself? If they did form part of the original 'libelli' then Connolly's suggestions have something to commend them. But if not, then his lines of interpretation must be abandoned in favour of those of Probst, Buchwald, and others.

From the manuscript it is very difficult to say whether the signs did form an original part of the 'libelli'; there are no means of making an unequivocal decision. It may, however, be suggested that, if not in the case of others, then at least as has occurred with the letters P SP F E in the margin following formula 358, it is not unlikely that such notes were added by the compiler himself. The very fact of there not being any method or system in the employment of such signs only reflects what has been found to be true of the book as a whole. As we have already seen, Lowe has suggested that such signs are to be taken as cross-references to the archetype. If by this he means the material in the possession of the compiler, then the sug-gestion cannot be dismissed as wholly impossible. But once again any clear evidence is lacking.

Perhaps the most fruitful approach and the one which has most convincingly explained the notes is that of Andrieu; it is basically this interpretation that Mohlberg[1] follows. But even this theory is not entirely without difficulties, and certain changes have been proposed in the arrangement of the formulae in order that the

---

[1] Mohlberg, op. cit., pp. xxvi and xxix (note d).

interpretation should be preserved. It may be possible to interpret the notes in a more liberal fashion. If we accept P = 'prex', then it is not necessary to press that 'prex' = 'proper preface' exclusively; this brings difficulties—as it has in the case of the theory which Andrieu proposes. If the term 'prex' is taken simply to mean 'prayer', 'formula', then perhaps the abbreviations will be rather more intelligible. Thus we conclude that these notes have, in all probability, been added by the compiler of the collection (as a sort of shorthand, in order to indicate that a formula is missing in any particular set), and that they point out that the missing formula is one which has already been used. Alternatively, it may be that an extemporized prayer is required at this stage. Further than this it is difficult to proceed on the evidence we have. No line of interpretation has yet been found to be entirely consistent and therefore satisfactory.

APPENDIX B

ON *CURSUS* IN THE LEONINE SACRAMENTARY

AFTER careful examination, it may be asserted that the prayers of the Leonianum are written in neither verse nor prose; rather are they written in what may be termed 'rhythmic prose'. The final clauses[1] of the majority of these prayers appear not to have been written in a purely arbitrary way, but in a combination of words specially designed beforehand and fixed according to particular rules. Similarly, the prayers of the other two ancient Roman sacramentaries, the Gelasian and Gregorian, have a large number of endings which suggest that they too have been influenced by the same literary principle. This combination of language and rhythm in a particular way, known as *cursus*, was a definite feature of Roman liturgical compositions from sometime in the fourth century until the early part of the seventh.

Vacandard[2] suggests that the *cursus* became the rule so far as the papal chancery was concerned during the pontificate of Siricius (384–98) and that it disappeared after Gregory the Great (590–604); however, in the case of liturgical formulae, this same feature appears a little earlier (c. A.D. 350) and prevails until about the middle of the seventh century.

[1] Although many of the remarks in this note are particularly concerned with *cursus* in regard to the final clauses of the various formulae, this same feature does also occur not infrequently (perhaps two or three times in one prayer or sentence) at the end of phrases, e.g. formula 659:

Presta famulis tuis, domine, abundantiam protectiónis et grátiae	(tardus)
Da salutem méritis et córporis	(tardus)
Da continuae prosperitátis auménta	(planus)
et tibi semper fac ésse devótos	(planus)

Note also that this is still to be found in the Latin originals of the collects in the Book of Common Prayer, e.g. collect for Epiphany IV:

Deus qui nos in tantis periculis constitutos pro humana scis fragilitate non pósse subsístere	(tardus)
da nobis salutem méntis et córporis	(tardus)
ut ea quae pro peccatis nostris patiamur te adiuvánte vincámus	(planus)

[2] E. Vacandard, 'Le cursus: son origine, son histoire, son emploi dans la liturgie', *Revue des questions historiques*, 78 (Paris, 1905), pp. 59–102. See also H. Leclercq, 'Cursus' in *D.A.C.L.* iii, cols. 3193 ff.

Following a close study of the formulae of the Leonianum, Wilson[1] reaches two main conclusions. He suggests (1) that the final phrases of the prayers within the Leonianum are regulated by a metrical system which is for the most part strictly observed, and (2) that a large majority of the final phrases are instances of one or other of the three principal forms of the early *cursus*. His assertion is then that most of the rhythmic endings of the Leonianum correspond to one of the three main types of *cursus*—planus, tardus, or velox.

In an article written some years earlier than Wilson's, Dom Mocquereau,[2] anxious to illustrate the scrupulous way in which the compilers of liturgical prayer observed the rules of *cursus* during the fourth to the sixth centuries, examined closely the prayers of the Leonianum in this respect. He enumerates about 1030 clausulae with metrical endings from the Sacramentary, of which only ten did not conform in some way or another to the type of *cursus* we have noted to be prevalent during this period. It is quite clear from the detailed results of Mocquereau's study that there is a definite predominance of the planus ending in the Leonianum. One important consideration at this point is the fact that Pope Leo in his own writings favours the planus ending; the obvious conclusion is that Leo therefore composed the prayers which have the planus ending— Bianchini[3] was correct in attributing most of the material within the Sacramentary to Leo. But such a conclusion is highly questionable for a number of reasons. If we go on to note the distribution of the three major cadences in the Gelasian and Gregorian Sacramentaries, the same general feature begins to emerge, namely, the definite predominance of the planus ending. It would be very unreasonable on this ground alone to assert Leonine authorship for both of these. It may well be that the predominance of the planus ending in the Leonianum is no more than an imitation of Leo's style. Again, if, as appears to be the case, the principles of the *cursus* were a definite literary feature of the papal chancery and also of the Roman liturgical compositions from the mid fourth century, then it may even be suggested that on these grounds there need not be any direct and particular relation between the writings of Leo and the prayers of the Sacramentary, but that both Leo's own literary style and the Leonine prayers are the product of a centre where the planus ending was for one reason or another most commonly used. In any case, the existence of this or that rhythmic ending does not and cannot of itself point to any particular author. However, when authorship has

---

[1] H. A. Wilson, 'The Metrical Endings of the Leonine Sacramentary', *J.T.S.* 5 (1904), pp. 386–95; 6 (1905), pp. 381–91.
[2] *Paléographie musicale*, iv (Solesmes), pp. 36 ff.
[3] See above, pp. 10–11.

been established on other grounds—style, theological or historical content—such information can serve to establish more forcefully arguments which already exist.

What then is the value of an examination of the occurrence of *cursus* in the formulae of the Leonianum? It is necessary to draw out the implications of the assertion that the existence of *cursus* supports and establishes more fully arguments already put forward on other grounds. Most of the material within the Sacramentary can be assigned to a period from about the mid fourth century to the latter part of the sixth;[1] all the indications are that this material originated in Rome;[2] much of it has been attributed to various popes.[1] These various conclusions have been reached on criteria other than *cursus*. However, when considering *cursus* in relation to the prayers of the Leonianum, these are considerably strengthened and more firmly established. It would indeed be astonishing if so large a number as 1030 clausulae with rhythmic endings were not to be found within the Leonianum. It is interesting in this respect to note that Wilson describes the material of the Sacramentary as giving 'an impression of uniformity rather than of difference—of such uniformity as might be found on the one hand in a collection of material composed by different writers guided as to the forms of their phrases by a common usage, or on the other in a collection of forms which may have been gathered from different sources or based on material of different dates, but which have for the most part been subjected to revision by a single hand'. It is possible to say then that so far as *cursus* is concerned, there is a certain 'uniformity' about the Leonianum. Not only is all the material within the Sacramentary to be dated within the bounds of the period in which *cursus* flourished as a literary feature of Roman liturgical compositions, but also it is asserted that the material has that centre as its place of origin. Further, it has been shown that the number of papal contributions is considerable.

Quite rightly Willis[3] states that the presence of rhythmic endings is useless for dating a document within the period when it is known *cursus* was a common literary device. Thus, since almost all the material within the Leonine Sacramentary was produced in precisely that period, it would come as something of a surprise if there were no evidence of *cursus* in most of the formulae. In addition, a detailed study of the Sacramentary has led to the conclusion that the material is very closely associated with Rome, its people, its history, and its popes, and certainly the papal contributions to the collection of

---

[1] See above, p. 117.   [2] See above, pp. 135 ff.

[3] G. G. Willis, 'Essays in Early Roman Liturgy', *Alcuin Club Collection*, no. 46 (London, 1964), p. 113.

liturgical material in the Sacramentary are by no means negligible. These conclusions have undoubtedly been reinforced by the researches of Dom Mocquereau and others into the existence of *cursus* and the very prominent part it played in the literary productions of the Roman church over a period of three hundred years or so.

BIBLIOGRAPHY

Editions of the Leonine Sacramentary:

BIANCHINI, J., *Anastasii Bibliothecarii—Vitae Romanorum Pontificum*, vol. 4 (Rome, 1735), cols. xii–lvii.

MURATORI, L. A., *Liturgia Romana Vetus*, vol. 1 (Venice, 1748), cols. 293–484.

ASSEMANI, J. A., *Codex Liturgicus Ecclesiae Universae*, vol. 4 (Rome, 1754), pp. 1–180.

BALLERINI, P., *Sancti Leonis Magni Romanis Pontificis Opera*, vol. 2 (Venice, 1756), pp. 1–160.

MIGNE, J. P., *Patrologia Latina*, vol. 55, cols. 22–156 (Ballerini text).

FELTOE, C. L., *Sacramentarium Leonianum* (Cambridge, 1896).

MOHLBERG, L. C., *Sacramentarium Veronense*, Rerum Ecclesiasticarum Documenta, Series Maior, Fontes I (Rome, 1956).

Other Liturgical Texts:

Sacramentarium Gelasianum, ed. L. C. Mohlberg, Liber Sacramentorum Romanae Aeclesiae Ordinis anni circuli (Cod. Vat. Reg. 316 / Paris, Bibl. Nat. 7193, 41/56), Rerum Ecclesiasticarum Documenta, Series Maior Fontes IV (Rome, 1960).

The Gregorian Sacramentary, ed. H. A. Wilson (Henry Bradshaw Society, London, 1915).

Das Sacramentarium Gregorianum nach dem Aachener Urexemplar (this is claimed to be the original text of the Sacramentary as sent by Hadrian to Charlemagne; the reconstruction is based upon the manuscript Cambrai 164), ed. H. Lietzmann, Liturgiegeschichtliche Quellen, vol. 3 (Münster i. W., 1921).

Die älteste erreichbare Gestalt des Liber Sacramentorum anni circuli der römischen Kirche (the text is claimed to be pre-Hadrianic and is based on the manuscript Padua D. 47), ed. L. C. Mohlberg, O.S.B., and A. Baumstark, Liturgiegeschichtliche Quellen, vols. 11 and 12 (Münster i. W., 1927).

The Bobbio Missal, ed. E. A. Lowe (Henry Bradshaw Society, liii, lviii, 1917–20); with notes and studies by A. Wilmart, O.S.B., E. A. Lowe, H. A. Wilson (Henry Bradshaw Society, lxi, 1924).

Missale Gothicum, ed. L. C. Mohlberg, (Cod. Vat. Reg. 317) Rerum Ecclesiasticarum Documenta, Series Maior, Fontes V (Rome, 1961).

Missale Francorum, ed. L. C. Mohlberg, (Cod. Vat. Reg. 257) Rerum Ecclesiasticarum Documenta, Series Maior, Fontes II (Rome, 1957).

The Stowe Missal, ed. G. F. Warner, 2 vols. (Henry Bradshaw Society, London, 1906, 1915).

The Rosslyn Missal, ed. H. J. Lawlor (Henry Bradshaw Society, London, 1899).

Books and Articles:

ANDRIEU, M., 'Les sigles du sacramentaire léonien', *Revue bénédictine*, 42 (1930), pp. 127–35.

BATIFFOL, P., 'Christum in cubile', *Revue biblique*, 3 (1894), pp. 437–8.
—— *Cathedra Petri* (Paris, 1938).
BAUMSTARK, A., *Liturgie comparée* (Chevetogne, 1940), new edn. by B. Botte, O.S.B., 1953; Eng. edn. by F. L. Cross, 1958.
BISHOP, E., *Liturgica Historica* (Oxford, 1918).
BOURQUE, E., *Étude sur les sacramentaires romains*, vol. 1, 'Les textes primitifs' (Rome, 1948).
BRUYLANTS, P., O.S.B., *Concordance verbale du sacramentaire léonien* (extract from Archivum Latinitatis Medii Aevi, 18–19, Brussels, 1945–8), Louvain.
BUCHWALD, R., 'Das sogennante Sacramentarium Leonianum und sein Verhältnis zu den beiden andern römischen Sakramentarien', *Weidenauer Studien*, 2 (1908), pp. 187–251.
CALLEWAERT, C., 'S. Léon le Grand et les textes du léonien', *Sacris Erudiri*, i (1948), pp. 36–164.
CAPELLE, B., O.S.B., 'Messes du pape S. Gélase dans le sacramentaire léonien', *Revue bénédictine*, 56 (1945–6), pp. 12–41.
CHADWICK, H., 'St. Peter and St. Paul in Rome; The Problem of the Memoria Apostolorum Ad Catacumbas', *Journal of Theological Studies*, 8 (1957), pp. 31–52.
CHAVASSE, A., 'Messes du pape Vigile dans le sacramentaire léonien', *Ephemerides Liturgicae*, 64 (1950), pp. 161–213; 66 (1952), pp. 145–219.
COEBERGH, C., 'S. Gélase premier auteur principal du soi-disant sacramentaire léonien', *Ephemerides Liturgicae*, 64 (1950), pp. 214–37.
—— 'S. Gélase premier auteur de plusieurs messes et prières du sacramentaire léonien', *Ephemerides Liturgicae*, 65 (1951), pp. 171–81.
—— 'S. Gélase premier auteur de plusieurs messes et préfaces du soi-disant sacramentaire léonien', *Sacris Erudiri*, 4 (1952), pp. 46–102.
—— 'Saint Léon le Grand auteur de la grande formule "Ad virgines sacras" du sacramentaire léonien', *Sacris Erudiri*, 6 (1954), pp. 282–326.
CONNOLLY, H., 'On some of the "notae" in the Leonine Sacramentary', *Revue bénédictine*, 38 (1926), pp. 196–204.
CROSS, F. L., 'Pre-Leonine Elements in the Proper of the Roman Mass', *Journal of Theological Studies*, 50 (1949), pp. 191–7.
CULLMANN, O., *Peter—Disciple, Apostle, Martyr*, Eng. edn. by F. V. Filson (London, 1953).
DE BEER, R., 'Bemerkungen über den ältesten Handschriftenbestand des Klosters Bobbio', *Sitzungsberichte* of the Vienna Academy, Philos.-hist. Classe, 1911, no. 11, pp. 89–90.
DELEHAYE, H., *Les Origines du culte des martyrs* (2nd edn., Brussels, 1933).
DE PUNIET, *Le Pontifical romain* (Louvain–Paris, 1930; Eng. trans. by M. V. Harcourt, London, 1932).
DIX, G., O.S.B., *The Apostolic Tradition of Hippolytus* (London, 1937).
—— *The shape of the liturgy* (2nd edn., London, 1954).
DOLD, A., and WÖLFLE, M., *Sacramentarium Leonianum* (Beuron, 1957).
DUCHESNE, L., *Le liber pontificalis*, 2 vols. (Paris, 1886–92).
—— *Origines du culte chrétien* (1889), Eng. trans. by M. L. McClure with the title *Christian Worship* (London, 1903).

—— *L'Histoire ancienne de l'Église chrétienne*, 3 vols. (Paris, 1906–10), Eng. trans., *The Early History of the Church*, 3 vols. (1909–24).

DUFOURCQ, A., *De manichaeismo apud Latinos quinto sextoque seculo, atque de Latinis apocryphis libris* (Paris, 1900).

FRERE, W. H., *Studies in Early Roman Liturgy*, 1. 'The Kalendar' (Alcuin Club Collection, Oxford–London, 1930).

GAMBER, K., 'Sakramentartypen', *Texte und Arbeiten*, 49/50 (1958), p. 48.

—— *Codices Liturgici Latini Antiquiores* (Freiburg, Schw.), 1963, pp. 110–11, no. 601.

HANSON, R. P. C., 'The Liberty of the Bishop to improvise prayer in the Eucharist', *Vigiliae Christianae*, 15 (1961), pp. 173–6.

HARRISON, O. G., 'The formulas "Ad virgines sacras". A study of the sources', *Ephemerides Liturgicae*, 66 (1952), pp. 252–73.

HURTER, H., S.J., *Nomenclator litterarius*, 4 vols. (Innsbruck, 1895).

JAFFÉ, P., *Regesta Pontificum Romanorum*, 2 vols. (Leipzig, 1885–8).

JUNGMANN, J. A., S.J., *The Mass of the Roman Rite* (American edn. New York, vol. i, 1951, vol. 2, 1955).

KENNEDY, V. L., *The Saints of the Canon of the Mass* (Studi di antichità cristiana, xiv, 1938).

KÜNG, H., *The Living Church* (London, 1953).

KUYPERS, A. B., *The Prayer Book of Edwald the Bishop commonly called the Book of Cerne* (Cambridge, 1902); liturgical note by E. Bishop, pp. 234 ff.

LEJAY, P., 'Le sacramentaire véronais, chronique de littérature chrétienne', *Revue d'histoire et de littérature religieuses*, 2 (1897), pp. 190–2.

LIETZMANN, H., 'Zur Datierung des Sacramentarium Leonianum', *Jahrbuch für Liturgiewissenschaft*, 2 (1922), pp. 101–2.

—— 'Petrus und Paulus in Rom', *Arbeiten zur Kirchengeschichte* (ed. 2, 1927), pp. 30–5.

LOWE, E. A., *Codices Latini Antiquiores*, vol. iv (Oxford, 1947).

MABILLON, J., *Vetera Analecta*, vol. i (Paris, 1675).

MORIN, G., O.S.B., 'La basilique dédiée à saint Pierre par le pape Symmaque sur la "via Trivana" à xxvii milles de Rome', *Bulletin d'ancienne littérature et d'archéologie chrétienne*, i (1911), pp. 241–6.

MURATORI, L. A., *Rerum Italicarum Scriptores*, vol. ii, pt. 2 (Milan, 1723).

NEUNHEUSER, B., 'In memoriam L. C. Mohlberg, O.S.B.', *Ephemerides Liturgicae*, 78 (1964), pp. 58–62.

PROBST, F., 'Duchesne, "über die drei ältesten römischen Sakramentarien"', *Zeitschrift für katholische Theologie*, 15 (1891), pp. 198–213.

—— *Die ältesten römischen Sakramentarien und Ordines* (Münster, 1892).

RAMSAY, W. M. *The Church in the Roman Empire* (London, 1893).

RANKE, E., *Das kirchliche Perikopsystem* (Berlin, 1847).

RULE, M., 'The Leonine Sacramentary; An analytical study', *Journal of Theological Studies*, 9 (1908), pp. 515–56; 10 (1909), pp. 54–99.

SAUER, F., *Sacramentarium Leonianum* (Codices selecti phototypice impressi, vol. 1, Graz, 1960).

STUIBER, A., 'Libelli Sacramentorum Romani', *Theophaneia*, 6 (Bonn, 1950).

TELFER, W., 'The Verona Codex LX (58)', *Harvard Theological Review*, 36 (1943), pp. 169–246.

TRAUBE, L., *Vorlesungen und Abhandlungen*, vol. i (Munich, 1909).

TURNER, C. H., 'An Arian Sermon from a ms. in the Chapter Library of Verona', *Journal of Theological Studies*, 13 (1911–12), pp. 19–21.

VAN KOSTEREN, 'Christum in cubile', *Revue biblique*, 4 (1895), pp. 65–6.

WARREN, F. E. *The Liturgy and Ritual of the Celtic Church* (Oxford, 1881).

WILSON, H. A., 'The Metrical Endings of the Leonine Sacramentary', *Journal of Theological Studies*, 5 (1904), pp. 386–95; 6 (1905), pp. 381–91.

The sacrament of Holy Orders (some papers and discussions concerning Holy Orders at a session of the Centre de Pastorale Liturgique, 1955), London, 1962.

'Constitutio De Sacra Liturgia' (Acta Ap. Sedis, 56 [1964], 97–134), *Ephemerides Liturgicae*, 78 (1964), pp. 185 ff.

INDEX